On the Vineyard II

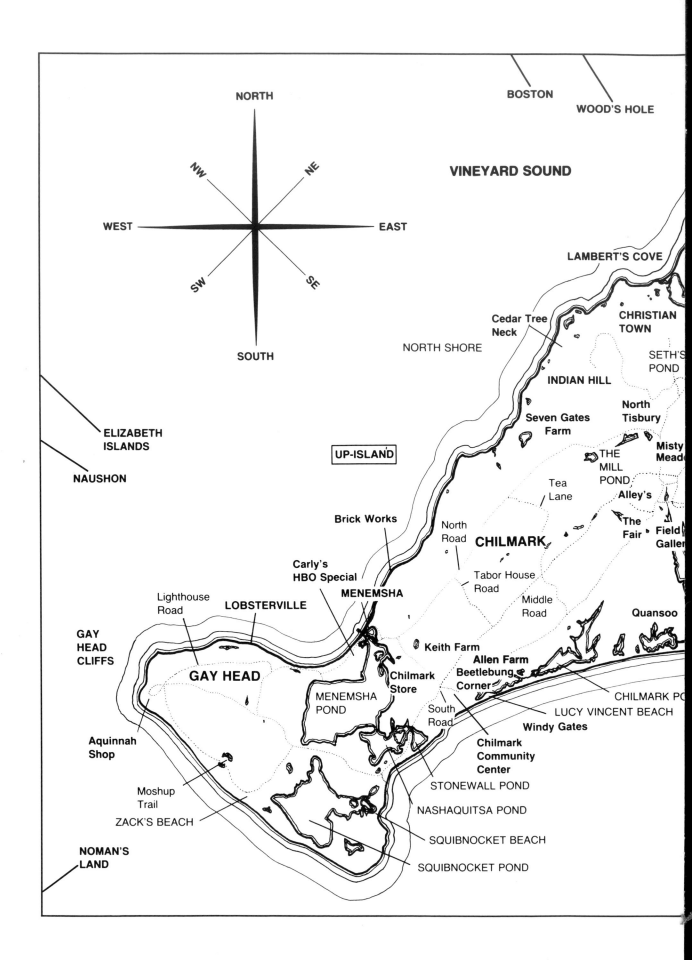

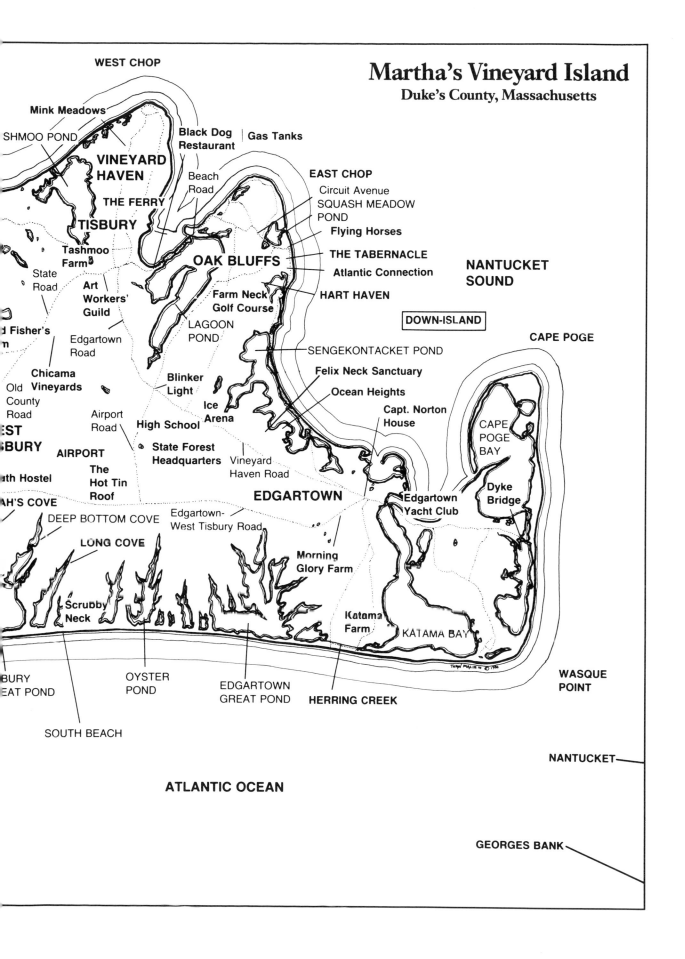

Martha's Vineyard Island
Duke's County, Massachusetts

WEST CHOP

Mink Meadows

SHMOO POND

VINEYARD HAVEN

Black Dog Restaurant | Gas Tanks

Beach Road

THE FERRY

TISBURY

Tashmoo Farm

State Road

Art Workers' Guild

Fisher's

Edgartown Road

Chicama Vineyards

Old County Road

EST BURY

Airport Road

High School

AIRPORT

The Hot Tin Roof

th Hostel

AH'S COVE

DEEP BOTTOM COVE

LONG COVE

Scrubby Neck

BURY
AT POND

OYSTER POND

SOUTH BEACH

EDGARTOWN GREAT POND

EAST CHOP

Circuit Avenue

SQUASH MEADOW POND

Flying Horses

THE TABERNACLE

Atlantic Connection

HART HAVEN

OAK BLUFFS

Farm Neck Golf Course

LAGOON POND

Blinker Light

Ice Arena

State Forest Headquarters

Vineyard Haven Road

EDGARTOWN

Morning Glory Farm

Katama Farm

KATAMA BAY

HERRING CREEK

SENGEKONTACKET POND

Felix Neck Sanctuary

Ocean Heights

Capt. Norton House

DOWN-ISLAND

NANTUCKET SOUND

CAPE POGE

CAPE POGE BAY

Dyke Bridge

Edgartown Yacht Club

WASQUE POINT

NANTUCKET

ATLANTIC OCEAN

GEORGES BANK

On the Vineyard II

with photographs by Peter Simon

and written contributions by Nancy Slonim Aronie, Barbara Lazear Ascher, Susan Branch, Robert Brustein, Art Buchwald, Douglas Cabral, James P. Comer, Philip R. Craig, Walter Cronkite, Ram Dass, Stephen Davis, Jib Ellis, Peter Feibleman, James S. Gordon, Lisa Grunwald, James Hart, Stan Hart, John Hough, Jr., Ward Just, Jim Kaplan, Gerald R. Kelly, Richard Lourie, Eileen Maley, Phyllis Méras, Victor Pisano, Robert Post, Arnie Reisman, Dionis Coffin Riggs, Jay Sapir, Anne W. Simon, Carly Simon, Richard C. Skidmore, William Styron, John Updike, Mike Wallace, Harvey Wasserman, Joel Zoss

Simon Press, RFD Box 280, Chilmark, MA 02535

All text copyrighted by the individual authors. We gratefully acknowledge permission to reprint:

"On Solitude" by Barbara Lazear Ascher, from *The Habit of Loving* (Random House), 1989.

"Going Barefoot" by John Updike, from *Hugging The Shore* (Alfred A. Knopf), 1983.

"Observations On a Nude Beach" by Richard Lourie, originally published, in a slightly different form, in *Boston Magazine*, 1983.

"A Journey Home" by John Hough, Jr., originally printed in the *Vineyard Gazette* in 1980, revised for *On the Vineyard II* in 1990.

"Housebroken" by Peter Feibleman, originally published in *Lears*, 1989.

"Never Been Gone" by Carly Simon and Jacob Brackman from the song by the same name that appears on the album *Spy*.

"Fisherman's Song" and "We Just Got Here" are song lyrics from the record *Happy Birthday* by Carly Simon.

Photo credits: All photographs by Peter Simon, except p. 41 (top) photo courtesy of *The Martha's Vineyard Historical Society* and p. 101— Alison Shaw; Back Cover—Ronni Simon; hand coloring from black and white photographs on pp. 18, 45, 48, 108, 115 (top), 136—Ronni Simon.

ISBN: 0-9626285-0-6
Book designed by Peter Simon.
Set in 24-point Erhardt and 10-point Trump Mediaeval by C&C Associates, Wilmington, MA.
Printed by Kirkwood Publications, Wilmington, MA.

First printing, May 1990

Published by Simon Press, RFD Box 280, Chilmark, MA 02535, (508) 645-9575.

Dedication and Acknowledgements

On the Vineyard II is a collaborative effort by many of us who live here. It is dedicated to the preservation of our land, sea, natural resources, and lifestyle. I wish to deeply thank all the authors who were generous enough to contribute their work to this anthology. In addition, I'd like to give thanks and praise to various others who have aided greatly in this project:

Ronni Simon, my creative and supportive wife, who helped me edit the photographs as well as the manuscripts. Ronni is a key source of advice and inspiration for me.

Douglas Cabral, editor of *The Martha's Vineyard Times*, who spent many hours toiling with the text, editing and proofreading, far and beyond the call of friendship.

Kirk Safford of C&C Associates. His company is responsible for the fine design and production of this book, and Kirk worked long and hard to make sure all the numbers made sense and that the various deadlines were all met along the way.

Gerry Davidson, also of C&C Associates, lent her extraordinary expertise with high-tech computer layouts and composition, and helped immeasurably with the design and flow of *On the Vineyard II*. We kept some long hours together. Also, **Darlene Bacheller** was very helpful with her attention to detail at the copy-editing stage.

Laura Joseph, Thaw Malin, Jackie Clason, Cecil Johnson, Richard Skidmore and **Joan LeLacheur** all gathered at our home one long night in the middle of the winter to help whittle down an inordinate number of color transparencies to the final ones that made it. And special thanks to Thaw Malin for providing the map of the Vineyard.

Bob McMahon, Island television producer extraordinaire, contributed supplementary material to enhance a few of the essays.

Jim Hart, over long distance telephone, was helpful in suggesting where certain articles could be changed and improved upon.

Ann Nelson, proprietor of the *Bunch of Grapes* bookstore and **Dana Anderson**, owner of *Bickerton & Ripley of Edgartown*, gave me marketing and format guidance.

And finally, *The Martha's Vineyard Times* and *Vineyard Gazette*, where many of these photographs (at least the black and white) first appeared. Over the past sixteen years these two Island newspapers have provided me with inspiration and a forum for producing these images.

Contents

Another opening, another show.

An Introduction

BY PETER SIMON

In July of 1980 the first edition of *On the Vineyard* was published by Doubleday. After four successful years, the book went out of print. Bookstores on the Island reported to me that many customers were still clamoring for it. From time to time I would receive a phone call from someone saying in a slightly desperate tone of voice, "I know the book is out of print now, but do you have any of your own copies left to sell? I'm willing to pay more . . ." Alas, I was down to my final dog-eared few.

Several years passed, and I still kept getting calls and letters asking for *On the Vineyard*. Having gained some publishing experience by producing *The Vineyard Calendar*, I approached Doubleday about buying the rights and the original materials in order to reprint it myself. Doubleday agreed to let me have it for a small fee, but then couldn't locate the "films" as they are called in the publishing arena. Undaunted, I realized that I could simply publish a brand new version, and the new book would serve as a nice complement to volume one.

The next step was to approach some of the same writers who appeared in the first edition, plus many new authors who had developed and gained recognition over the past ten years. I wanted to see if there was still a willingness to participate on the same basis—that is, to contribute their essays for free since a significant portion of the book's profits would be going to an Island charity. I entered the procurement phase cautiously. After all, it was the late eighties now, not the altruistic seventies. After eight years of Ronald Reagan, I figured people were looking out for number one more than ever, and would slough me off with comments like, "I'd love to, but I've got three imposing deadlines and I'm way behind."

But to my delight, almost everyone was willing to contribute something. A few even expressed a sense of honor that I had asked! I was filled with a feeling of oneness about our little community that reminded me, once again, why it is that we choose to live here. I doubt I could have gotten a similar response were I trying to publish a book about a place like New Haven or Palm Beach. That all these authors, many of them with international reputations, took the time and energy to contribute still has me floating.

Choosing a suitable Island charity proved the most difficult decision. There are so many worthy causes here—Martha's Vineyard Community Services (a portion of the first book's profits went there), The Boys and Girls Club, The Historical Preservation Society, The Ice Arena, The Red Stocking Fund, just to name a few. But when confronted with a life and death situation—the ultimate bottom line—we turn to the Martha's Vineyard Hospital to have our most pressing needs met. And as many of us who live here know, the hospital is in dire straits. The hospital budget is weakened by delayed or underpaid Medicare reimbursements and increased medical costs. Additionally, there is an ongoing need for updated equipment and expansion. The hospital is trying to raise more than five million dollars for an endowment fund which could secure its financial stability into the next century and beyond. Our community needs a reliable and first class

Everything seemed funny back in the late 60's.

facility, so whatever funds may be generated through the sale of this book will help bring the hospital a little closer to that goal.

As the articles poured in, I began matching the many photographs I have taken here through the years to the text. In certain cases I had to go out and take new shots to help illustrate the text more specifically. I also gave some authors particular topics to ensure that the pieces all fit together like a jigsaw puzzle, with as few overlaps as possible. It obviously was impossible to touch on or include photographs of everything noteworthy—there are so many different lives, settings and subcultures that could be written about. But what emerged, just like a print from the developing tray in my darkroom, were personal, highly emotional and strikingly dissimilar accounts of what Vineyard life means to all these different observers—a tapestry of interconnected existences. And what resulted from these distinctly singular accounts is a surprisingly complete picture. The intent is to portray a reasonably balanced, realistic

view; focusing on the unique charm and alluring qualities of the Island, but not ignoring such problems as overdevelopment, an undependable economy, and limited horizons for the year-rounder. For the reader my hope is that, given the breadth of these essays, some, if not most, will ring true.

Many of the essays in this book evoke some of my special feelings about the Vineyard. For example, I share with Mike Wallace his particular feeling of "roots." Even though I grew up in New York City, I came here many summers with my family, and slowly developed the ties that bind. I became, in 1969, one of the "boomers" that Gerry Kelly outlines in his essay. I found the rural lifestyle mixed with the majestic oceanscapes and alternative values, environmental awareness, and artistic endeavors hard to resist. The Vineyard seemed to encourage sophisticated yet informal behavior, and tolerated a variety of diametrically opposed ways of life. I, for one, developed a summer habit of never wearing shoes if I could help it. I was amazed to find how few people

2

objected. It seems the proper metaphor for John Updike, as he addresses the subject in his essay "Going Barefoot." Finally, in 1973, I bought a shack in Gay Head. I was merely a summer and "shoulder season" resident back then, carefully balancing a career-oriented off-Island life, with an Island summer euphoria of sun, waves, grass, softball, romance, music and grace, with an occasional photograph mixed in between.

Slowly, the pull of the big city released its grasp. I grew to enjoy the life in a smaller pond, and felt overwhelmed and claustrophobic surrounded by tall buildings and the harshly competitive lives stuck within. I became too keenly aware of the growing disparity between the rich and the poor. John Hough, Jr. describes the city/country ambivalence passionately in his essay "A Journey Home." In New York success was measured, it seemed to me, by income, who you knew, what parties you had access to, what clothes you wore, and whether or not you arrived in a limo. All those trappings became less relevant to me as the years passed. By 1986, I was ready to "drown my ambitions in the sea" as my sister Carly writes, and move here year-round. My Gay Head shack became a Chilmark home, and there was a loving wife and red-haired son to share it all with. I had more time to spend with them, and less time stuck in traffic, waiting for elevators, and trying to make a big "deal" with someone behind a mammoth desk. It all began to make sense, finally. True, the stakes were smaller here, and the mountains were easier to climb, but the rewards are ultimately more meaningful. Stan Hart says it well in his essay: "I feel that I know everyone, and everyone knows me and that I am home and what I do here matters very much indeed."

And now when I go to the city I get my business done, visit my entertaining relatives, and touch down on a few old bases that used to mean so much: see an old friend who I have known since childhood, take a trip out to Shea Stadium to catch a Mets game, or check out a Neil Young concert at Radio City. But soon the call of the Island returns and draws me back, hurrying to make the ferry on time. It is so good to get away for a bit, but better to arrive home, with a new appreciation for having decided to make my headquarters here after all. Perhaps as the cities become increasingly inhumane with their drugs, violence, traffic and pollution, more people and their families will make the same move as I.

But all is not perfect. In mid-January I do question at times whether the isolation and hibernation is tolerable. The winter, for me, can be bleak; all the closed-down shops, only one movie a week, very little diversion or recreation. Islanders turn inward, and the home becomes the only place for entertainment. With a VCR and telephone at hand, life is reduced to the bare essentials. If only there were indoor tennis, a bowling alley and a place conducive to stimulating social interaction. Walter Cronkite's wish —that the summer wasn't so crowded and the winter so sparse, that things could even out a bit—hits home. I can imagine that eventually the year-round population will grow and evolve into a more stimulating, diverse community. With fax machines and computers, it's becoming possible to earn a living here pursuing a wide variety of endeavors.

By the time March rolls around, the ongoing psychodrama reaches a crescendo here. As Jim Gordon states in his article, substance abuse goes wild, and normally placid people find miscellaneous trivialities a cause for outbursts of uncontrolled anger. Winter on the Vineyard can be as lovely as a Phyllis Méras snow walk, but let's not ignore the downside. Life can be particularly rough for the teenagers who have little to do, and for their parents whose summer money has run out. With our economy based on the three or four months of tourists and summer people, it is hard for many to find ways to support themselves through the harsh winter months. Some Islanders, without kids or other responsibilities, flee to warmer spots. But once the nicer weather sets in, all the winter woes fade into the background. The shops and restaurants reopen

A new snow breaks the monotony of a Vineyard winter.

Hurricane-spawned swells draw out the small but hardy Island surfer contingent (above) and creates winds over 50 MPH for the launch of the annual windsurfing race at Menemsha Beach (right).

Queen Ann's lace, which grows in abundance all summer long, forms a swaying foreground for the Gay Head lighthouse (above).

Lobster pots and buoys with the Edgartown lighthouse in the distance.

5

When hurricane Gloria posed a threat to the Island in 1985, everything, including Main Street in Vineyard Haven, came to a halt. Typically, the storm sideswiped the Vineyard and bashed Long Island instead.

like the purple wisteria, all the familiar faces pop out of the woodwork, and we're back in the high life again.

The Island is at its best in June and September. June has all the breathtaking blooming flowers, the fresh shiny leaves on the trees, the aromatic outdoor air and all the anticipation, but less of the summer intensity that makes some year-rounders crazy. It was in June that Carly gave her memorable live performance in Gay Head (for her HBO special). It was a special event for Islanders. The summer residents had yet to arrive, and the audience was composed of a perfect combination of music/Carly/Island lovers who just couldn't believe such a magical event was unfolding. Carly, normally reluctant to sing before an audience, felt at home and comforted by the familiar and supportive faces dotting the Menemsha backdrop. Many people who were there tell me that it ranks high on their Vineyard list of all-time favorite memories. Mine too.

And in September, the weather still mild and the ocean still swimmable, the Vineyard becomes accessible once again. The summer fog and haze lift to reveal days of crisp horizons and cumulus-dotted skies, with a foreground of golden-rod and beach plums. The mosquitoes

and ticks of July and August relent, and the Island saves the best that it has to give for those who survived the summer. Being the ultimate weather freak, I find that September presents the greatest of possibilities. A hurricane moves up the coast and all attention turns to the weather maps and forecasts. As the storm approaches, the Island suddenly unifies into a single being; there is a communal sharing of preparation and helping each other out as we would ourselves. If the would-be hurricane misses, as most often it does, we breath a collective sigh of relief, but the ardent surfers have days of ecstatic utterances. Normal routine comes to a grinding halt as daylight hours are consumed by catching the perfect wave; our one chance a year to resemble the North Shore of Oahu. Always particularly prone to the ways of the weather, Vineyard activities are planned around the forecasts: from fishing excursions, golf games, cutting the hay, harvesting the grapes, wondering if today, in fact, will qualify as a "perfect 10" beach day, to deciding if the fog will lift so that the boats can run or if the winds will pick up enough for an afternoon sail or some windsurfing.

All this and more is what life on the Vineyard means to me. The pleasures seem never-ending and are constantly re-inventing themselves. Ram Dass once said to me, "You know, it never ceases to amaze me that the Vineyard doesn't get tired of appreciating itself." Once one puts in any amount of time here, one becomes gradually addicted. Eventually, living on the Vineyard becomes a passionate obsession, a religion, a personal identity and a raison d'être. I once overheard someone ask a friend what he does here for a living. He replied, "My job is to live here. The money takes care of itself." It is with this spirit of appreciation and celebration that the second volume of *On the Vineyard* is published.

Carly Simon performs live to a select audience at West Basin for her first HBO special in June, 1987.

A Menemsha sunset reflects off the windows of Carly's cottage.

Summer activity in full swing at the Tisbury town dock.

In Praise Of Vineyard Haven

BY WILLIAM STYRON

Once at a summer cocktail party in Menemsha I was asked by a lady: "Where on the Island do you live?" "In Vineyard Haven," I replied. She suddenly gave me a look that made me feel as if I harbored a communicable disease. "My God," she said, "I didn't think anyone *lived* there."

Well, people do live there, and the moment of the year that I look forward to with unsurpassed anticipation is when I roll the car off the ferry, negotiate the fuss and confusion of the dock area, wheel my way past the homely facade of the A & P, twist around down Main Street with its (let's face it) unprepossessing ranks of mercantile emporia, and drive northward to the beloved house on the water. On an Island celebrated for its scenic glories, Vineyard Haven will never win a contest for beauty or charm; perhaps that's partly why I love it. The ugly duckling gains its place in one's heart by way of an appeal that is not immediately demonstrable. The business district is a little tacky, but why should it be otherwise? It is neither more nor less inspiring than other similar enclaves all across the land. People often think they yearn for quaintness, for stylishness, for architectural harmony; none of these would be appropriate to Vineyard Haven, which thrives on a kind of forthright frowsiness. A few years ago an overly eager land developer—now mercifully departed from the Island—was heard proclaiming his desire to transform downtown Vineyard Haven into a "historical" site, similar to the metamorphosis effected by Mr. Beinecke on Nantucket. It is good that this plan came to naught. How silly and dishonest Brickman's and Leslie's Drugstore would look wearing the fake trappings of Colonial Williamsburg.

As for residential handsomeness, the good town of Tisbury cannot compete with Edgartown—that stuffy place; even so, had the lady from Menemsha walked along William Street or viewed more closely some of the dwellings lining the harbor, she would have discovered houses of splendid symmetry and grace. She would have also found some of the noblest trees lining the streets of any town of its size on the Eastern Seaboard. It is this loose, amorphous "small townness" that so deeply appeals to me. A large part of the year I live in a rural area of New England where one must drive for miles to buy a newspaper. The moors of Chilmark and the lush fens of Middle Road then, despite their immense loveliness, do not lure me the way Vineyard Haven does. I like the small-town sidewalks and the kids on the bikes and the trespassing gangs of dogs and the morning walk to the post office past the Main Street Café, with its warm smell of pastry and coffee. I like the whole barefoot, chattering melee of Main Street—even, God help me, the gawking tourists with their Instamatics and their avoirdupois. I like the preposterous gingerbread bank and the local lady shoppers with their Down East accents, discussing *bahgins.*

Mostly I love the soft collision here of harbor and shore, the subtly haunting briny quality that all small towns have when they are situated on the sea. It is often manifested simply in the *sounds* of the place—sounds unknown to forlorn inland municipalities; even West Tisbury. To the stranger these sounds might

The Tisbury Town Hall.

The annual street fair in Vineyard Haven signals the advent of summer.

Horses and snow at Tashmoo Farm, only 2 miles from downtown.

10

appear distracting, but as a fussy, easily distracted person who has written three large books within earshot of these sounds, I can affirm that they do not annoy at all. Indeed, they lull the mind and soul, these vagrant noises; the blast of the ferry horn—distant, melancholy—and the gentle thrumming of the ferry itself outward bound past the breakwater; the sizzling sound of sailboat hulls as they shear the waves; the luffing of sails and the muffled boom of the yacht club's gun; the eerie wail of the breakwater siren in dense fog; the squabble and cry of gulls. And at night to fall gently asleep to the far-off moaning of the West Chop foghorn. And deep silence save for the faint *clink-clinking* of halyards against a single mast somewhere in the harbor's darkness. Vineyard Haven. Sleep. Bliss.

The well-appointed (and often photographed) Hine's Point lobster shack.

William Styron is the author of the much-lauded Sophie's Choice *(Random House). His other works include* Lie Down In Darkness, Set This House On Fire, The Long March, *and the Pulitzer Prize-winning novel* The Confessions Of Nat Turner. *He is currently working on a non-fiction book about depression. When not in his beloved Vineyard Haven he lives in Roxbury, Connecticut with his wife Rose, an activist and poet.*

William Styron with Cozzie, 1980.

Just another Menemsha sunset, where demented aliens gather to applaud.

Menemsha

BY ARNIE REISMAN

Menemsha. An old Native American word freely translated as "place where demented aliens gather to applaud the setting of the sun while eating supper in the sand." Or rather, that's what comes to mind in August. The rest of the year, thankfully, other translations bob tranquilly between my ears.

Menemsha. Like so much of this Island, this place is timeless. In more ways than one. There are hardly any clocks around here. You don't see them in the shops. You don't see them in the homes. The pace of life just doesn't run like that. Not to the incessant ticks and tocks of some judgmental supervisor. Not around here. Here you tell time the old fashioned way—you make it. The day is yours. Do with it what you will. When you're done, go to sleep.

This place is also timeless in a larger way. Take a picture of it. Any part of it. The wooden houses, the wooden fishing shacks, the wooden shops—the Galley, the Byte, the Deli, the Home Port, Poole's fish market, Larsen's fish market, the General Store. The water, the sand, the jetty. The dirt roads, the rocky roads, the paved roads. Doesn't make much difference when you take that picture. Just look at it and tell me when it was taken. Could have been today, right? Or could have been yesterday or last year or a decade ago or a generation ago or tomorrow. Oh, there would be a few telltale signs—new beams down at Dutcher Dock or new pumps at the Texaco station. Some cars and some boats would be giveaways—but even with them you'd still have to hedge your bets. Your safest reaction would be: "This picture was taken definitely some time after 1965.

Yep, definitely." Unless, of course, you were holding a photograph taken right after the Great Hurricane of 1938 swooped over the harbor. You'd be holding a photograph of the General Store with just about nothing around it.

If you were taking a photograph out in Menemsha fifty years ago, besides the great debris left by the Great Hurricane, you might have captured James Thurber trying to think of something funny while walking along North Road. He was the first person to tell me about Menemsha. Not in person, mind you. In a published collection of letters I read thirty years ago when I was a kid in high school. He seemed to live the perfect life to me—writing for the *New Yorker* and living in Manhattan, in Paris, in the countryside of Connecticut, on the island of Bermuda and on the Island of Martha's Vineyard in a romantic-sounding place called Menemsha.

The island of Manhattan was exotic enough for me. Growing up in Colorado, I relished reading about Thurber's summer excursions from the ballyhoo that was Broadway to the lullaby that was the Vineyard. It sounded like it took forever. The humorist and his wife would hire a cook and pack their bags for a month's vacation. Sometimes they packed up their lives for a whole summer. Then they'd all pile into a taxi and head off for New York's Pier 14. Once there, they'd board a ship called the Priscilla and meet their luggage in a little stateroom. About 5 in the afternoon they'd leave port. The next morning, some fifteen hours later, Priscilla would pull up her skirts on the shores of Fall River, Massachusetts. The Thurbers and the cook would disembark with their bags and take a taxi to New

Clearing before sunset.

Bedford. Once there, they'd board a smaller boat. This vessel would stop at Woods Hole to pick up freight and more passengers. The next stop was the Vineyard. Once there, the Thurber party would hire a car and head off to the cottage in Menemsha. When they had all settled in for rented relaxation without electricity, Thurber would work up one *New Yorker* story that would foot the bill for their time in this timeless place. As he once said to S. J. Perelman, displaying his knowledge of Yiddish, "it was well worth the schlep."

When my wife and I first bought a home in Menemsha, I called my mother in Denver to give her the good news and to invite her out. My mother had never been to this Island in her life. It was hard for her to comprehend why we would want to live in an antique frame house that any moment could go up in a blaze, thanks to one careless smoker or one misused match ("What's a matter, they got a law against bricks over there?"). It was hard for her to comprehend why such a catastrophe of a house would also be situated in a village surrounded by water that at any moment could get stormy and angry and drown you ("Your father worked and saved his whole life so we could move away from all the harsh elements and up into a high-rise."). It was even harder for her to comprehend the name of our little village.

"What's it called?" asked my mother, squinting to hear over the long-distance line.

"Menemsha," I said again. "It's actually a village in Chilmark. You've heard me talking about Chilmark. That's the town we rented that house in for all those years."

"Mushimshak?" She took a wild stab at it.

"Menemsha," I said again. "M-E-N-E-M-S-H-A."

"What kinda name is that, for heaven's sake?" Her voice seemed to question my intelligence. Like it wasn't enough that I bought a place that was God's gift to fires and floods, but it also sounded like you had to learn a new language to get along there.

"It's a Native American name," I said, trying to sound reasonable. "This was once part of Indian territory. A lot of this Island was. In fact, some of it still is."

"I'm glad to hear that. So, tell me, how far is it to drive from your real house to this place in Minoosha?"

Our "real house" was in the burbs outside Boston. We bought it right after we got married. It was not only our first adult house but also our only one until we bought the one in Menemsha, which we then renovated and winterized. So, as far as my wife and I are concerned, we have two real houses. One of them just sees us more often than the other. Which brings us back to my mother's question.

"It's not Minoosha, it's Menemsha," I continued. "Actually, it is a bit of a trip to get here. It takes about an hour and a half to drive to Woods Hole down at the Cape. That's where we get the ferry. You drive the car right onto this boat that holds 60 to 70 cars and off we go to the Vineyard. The ferry leaves about every hour and it takes about 45 minutes to cross the water. Then you dock in Vineyard Haven and . . ."

"Then you're home, after more than two hours of schlepping," my mother interrupted.

"Not exactly," I said, realizing I was now driving myself toward one of my mother's large psychological sink holes. "We still have another twelve miles of driving to do after we dock. You see, where we live is about 20 to 30 minutes from the ferry landing. But the whole adventure is real relaxing. I mean, it's not like you're driving the whole time. In the middle of the trip you get to stretch out on a boat. You can read, you can eat, you can just stare at the water. And the ride on the Island is very scenic, very restful too. You'll see when you get here."

"Whattayou talking about? I'm not coming there. By the time I got to your house. I'd need a real vacation."

"If you think that's a long trip," I said, "that's nothing." Then I told her about the way James Thurber got here. "Sounds like something out of a romance novel, huh?"

"Sounds like something out of the Depression," countered my mother.

"You're really going to like it. No matter when you come here, it feels refreshing. The air is crisp and clear. Sweet-smelling honeysuckle grows all over the place. There's no urban sprawl. There's no hustling around. There's no traffic jam. In fact, there's not much of a real road where we live. It's all dirt."

"Even downtown?"

"Menemsha doesn't have a downtown."

My mother digested this information along with my tone of voice. "You really like it, huh?"

"We love it."

"All right, I'll come. When I make up my mind when, I'll drop you a note. Give me your address."

"That's a quaint feature about this part of the Island. We don't have an address."

"Don't talk like an imbecile."

"I'm serious. There's a handful of street names, but most of them don't have signs, and none of the houses have numbers."

"How would anyone ever find your place?"

"We send them a map."

"What about Federal Express? How can they do their job?"

"Mother. I don't want to talk about Federal Express. I want to talk about Menemsha. I want to talk about your coming out here and seeing this wonderful place and staying with us in our new house. That's what I want to talk about. So, I want you to think about a date soon, because I've got to book the ferry."

"You gotta what?"

"You have to reserve your car space on the ferry in advance. When the weather gets warm, you have to book way in advance or you'd never get your car over. We have to book in February to make sure we get the dates we want for July."

"I never heard such a mishagas."

"That's why I want you to make up your mind real soon and call me."

"I don't know. Sounds like an awful lot. All this planning and booking and boating and driving. And all to go where? Some place that takes forever to get to. Some place in the dirt. Some place that's

Menemsha still life.

Menemsha by moonlight.

got no address! All this just to have a place all the way out in Godforsaken Meshugana!''

"It's Menemsha, not Meshugana!"

"That's what you say!"

Like always, she eventually believed me. She came, she saw, she was conquered. It was well worth the schlep.

Arnie Reisman, among other things, is a television writer and producer, was executive editor of The Boston Phoenix *and film critic for* Boston Magazine. *When he's not entertaining his mother at his Menemsha cottage, he lives in Wellesley, Massachusetts with his wife, Paula Lyons, consumer reporter for ABC-TV's* Good Morning America.

Menemsha by sunlight.

Wisteria Road, Gay Head.

On The Roads

BY RICHARD C. SKIDMORE

The total length of the twenty-one public roads on the Island is eighty miles. The space they occupy is pretty close to two-hundred and fifty-five acres of paved land, or four-tenths of one percent of the total area of the Island. These roads are a series of loops that curve to conform to the Island's silhouette. They have none of that straight-line-to-the-horizon quality that one associates with the open road. Here the roads are a closed system made finite by the water's edge.

They are pathways to the beauty of the Island, and by the way they wend, they direct our attention to the line of a particular stone wall or the lolloping descent of meadow to pond, or the surprise emergence of a view that skips forward from Nashaquitsa Pond to Menemsha Pond to the sea beyond—from land to water to land to water, a triple-glistening vista. Down-Island, the stretch of beach road between Edgartown and Oak Bluffs is thought by some to be one of the most beautiful roads in the world. Going toward Oak Bluffs, you have Nantucket Sound on your right, and Sengekontacket Pond, followed by Farm Pond on your left, for a total of almost three and three-quarters miles with water on both sides.

Though many Island roads display the beauty of the sea, the inland country charm of up-Island is best viewed on Middle and North roads. In summer they have a verdant allure that shimmers with the serenity of the past. The farms and woods and fields and overhanging trees conspire with the warmth of summer to produce a fairytale of pastoral peace. That fairytale is often obscured by the circus of summer celebration endured in the sacred name of seasonal economy.

The in-season roads teem with beach traffic—tour buses, bicycles, hitchhikers, all-variety of off-road vehicles, and, of course, the dread moped. At times, driving down-Island from Gay Head on that portion of South Road between Moshup Trail and Beetlebung Corner where there is only one narrow winding road, it is as if you were negotiating a mountain pass in Mexico, when around the curve ahead swings a tour bus half in your lane, heading for your car at forty or more miles-per-hour. The bus driver struggles to accommodate both the mopeders who have forced him out into your lane, and his schedule, which inhibits him from slowing down—thus raising moped inconvenience to a life-threatening situation.

In most cases the threat passes without incident, but in this particular case, something else happened which, even without mopeds, without the adrenalin, you might well have missed. If you were to run this mythical movie back in slow motion and watch the hand gripped on the wheel of the red Volvo station wagon behind the bus, you would see an index finger quickly rise and, just as quickly, flick down. Even in slow motion, the fast flickering first finger would seem inconsequential if you did not know the code of the year-rounders who infiltrate the roads of in-season.

Because summer only reigns for three months of the year, a case can be made that the off-season is the real Vineyard. But the year-round population of the real Vineyard is less than one-fifth of sum-

19

A display of local concerns.

off-season. By the end, your friends' cars, with their distinctive array of bumper stickers, scratches, dents, or in their glistening pristine-ness, are as well known, front and rear, as their drivers.

There is an extension of this ritual that—during the long, less hectic months of the secret season—seems quite natural. It usually occurs when the oncoming car you recognize belongs to someone you haven't run into lately at the market or post office, the PTA, AA, church, aerobics class, bridge or poker game. Rather than the finger salute, or wave, the full-scale flag down is employed, and both parties slow down, or back up, roll down their windows and chat. In the road. In off-season, this custom is well known, and a "do unto others" tolerance prevails—at times, up to six cars will wait quietly in any one direction. In season, year-rounders practicing the rite of conversation are lucky to get more than two-car tolerance before horns blow and off-Island heads and fists shake in the throes of consternation.

What is really going on here? Something quite ancient. From the *Oxford English Dictionary*: "Road: An ordinary line of communication used by persons passing between different places, usually one wide enough to admit of the passage of vehicles as well as of horses or travelers on foot." This sense of the word appeared in the late 1500's, a time when communication over any distance required movement. The Island is a small, far-flung community. Here, the roads themselves have not lost their ability to foster communication.

Lobsterville Road, Quansoo Road, Tiah's Cove Road—these are some of the names we come to know from Island driving, but as we trace and retrace the same routes, many more names are accumulated unconsciously. Surnames mostly—Nitchie, Montamat, Bettencourt, they click by. Sometimes they surface upon introduction. "Oh yes, are you the one with the pink mailbox on Middle Road?" Besides mailboxes, there are signs—the name Boyd with the picture of a bird painted next to it, or the

mer's droves, so even to veteran summer people, the off-season is largely unknown. It could be called the secret season. Which is where we find the source of road ritual.

In the environment of the secret season, the beaches recede in importance. Roads are traveled in pursuit of necessities—work or food or videos. Buses actually transport children to school rather than tourists to Gay Head. This time of year bird watching has nothing on car watching. You often drive for miles, especially up-Island, without seeing another car or truck. But when a vehicle does hover into sight, the year-rounder immediately scrutinizes the color, make, model, rust spots, and any other identifying characteristics, looking for clues to the identity of the approaching driver. In those last few feet before passing, having determined that "Yes, it is Jennifer," one has time to raise one's index finger from the steering wheel and receive an answering wave from Jennifer as she whizzes by.

Whether you give a greeting with your first finger, or a full-hand wave, is determined by your grip on the wheel. If you hold it at the top, chances are good that the finger salute is simplest and best. If you favor a side grip, then letting go with one hand and waving is most likely your style. For newcomers, all it takes is one small blue barrel with the house name painted on it. Or the trail marking signs on some of those two-mile dirt road driveways. Beware when the directions to the dinner party end with the words, "Then you just follow the yellow slash marks" or "Just follow the little mushrooms." It means navigating a sea of speed bumps, natural bumps, and the all-too-common ruts and rocks of an unknown road while trying not to miss the little purple-painted mushroom shapes.

Coming by car, only one road leads to Martha's Vineyard. That road ends at the floating parking lot known, generically, as "the ferry." In winter, more than ninety-five percent of the license plates of Island-bound cars and trucks read Massachusetts. In summer, every state in the Union sends a representative. Hawaii is a real head-turner. One summer delegate from Ohio has a plate with CHLMRK on it. This example of Vineyard devotion is a badge of entry to that old Island game: Who Loves The Vineyard More. You can be sure hundreds of Ohioians have wracked their brains trying to make the letters CHLMRK mean something. But, for its two months or so visit here, that

plate is full of meaning. In six letters it says Serious Summer Person.

Human schedules are sometimes, but not often, the same as ferry schedules. Sometimes you just have to leave the Island on short notice. Those are often the same sometimes that you find yourself in that non-mobile parking lot—the standby line. The standby line, for Island regulars, is its own subculture. Depending on the strictness of your travel plans, it is either a major, or slight inconvenience, literal hell, or mere purgatory. The most positive standby experiences are the ones when time is passed swiftly. Paradoxically, this is most likely to occur when the line is at its fullest.

To get the complete picture, a summer day when the boats, because of wind, or some such, can't dock in Oak Bluffs, provides a fine example. The standby line in Vineyard Haven then swells up to the population of a small Island town. The wanglers are out of their cars first, trying to get to the head of the line, using every ploy at their command. Family car discipline breaks down after the first hour of no motion, and youngsters start playing games on the hood while dad forages in the fast food shops, scouts the location of bathrooms and phones, and buys magazines for himself and the wife, comics for the kids. Meanwhile, the frisbees have

The standby line grows to mammoth proportions over Labor Day weekend . . .

. . . and there's nothin' left to do but smile, smile, smile.

For 5 years the annual Columbus Day "crunch" in Gay Head was a great place to say goodbye to a beloved Island car, but popular demand finally proved overwhelming for Hugh and Jeannie Taylor. The last demolition derby was held in 1982.

been flying for a while, and those who had expected to be going standby have their tailgate picnics set out. The more gregarious tailgates evolve into free-form salon buffets.

Often, friends and acquaintances turn out to be on the line and car hopping becomes a primary diversion along with going to the Black Dog Bakery for coffee and sweets. All in all, it begins to resemble some giant, impromptu, Fourth of July picnic or Grateful Dead concert parking lot. People and cars all waiting to get off.

The standby line is an opportunity to view Island road culture communication at a standstill. The predominance of *Save The Whales, Ban Mopeds, Vineyard Recycler,* and *No Nukes* bumper stickers is a quick straw poll of Island political concerns. *Living Sober* and *Martha Is Pro Choice* indicate our struggles. There are a staggering number of *Our Market* stickers that have been mutilated so that only the red and white map of the Vineyard is left. Some cars have an ostentatious display of yearly beach and dump stickers. Members of that status cult are judged by how many different town beach stickers they have for each year. A parlay of Philbin, Lucy Vincent and Lambert's Cove shows high rank, but even that is not always enough to avoid the notorious beach parking standby lines that have developed up-Island.

In Vineyard Haven, the standby line of summer traditionally shows a high proportion of Volvos. The Vineyard seems to be a regular stopping place in their migratory pattern. But conspicuous in its absence is that uniquely Vineyard vehicle, the Island car.

For those of us who live here year-round, or just own a house, the concept will be familiar. A car becomes an Island car at the precise moment you realize you do not feel it would be safe to go off-Island in it. Age is the primary factor, and the speed of off-Island might impart a higher level of vibration than is prudent. A chancy starter motor or solenoid, the slipping clutch, the nearly bald tires, the wobble in the steering, the fuel pump that must be tapped with a wrench—these are all the small annoyances that make you want to know for sure that no matter what happens, when it does, you won't be more than twenty miles from home or mechanic.

A Vineyard vehicle will pass among Islanders until it dies here—having been restricted, for its last years, to a diet of eighty miles of open road at forty or so miles per hour. The Island is a retirement home for ambulatory old vehicles—though for a few years, the demolition derby near the Gay Head cliffs provided a ritual of termination for Island cars whose owners favored bang over whimper.

Some years back, cabin fever struck a friend who had taken the car out for a quick run to the video store. It was about four p.m., nearing sunset, when a restless feeling seized her. She headed up-Island. Past Alley's her speed increased, the beautiful Island vistas became a blur. She got to the lighthouse in Gay Head in time for sunset but didn't stop. She just whipped around the loop and headed back down via Moshup Trail. When she returned hours later, feverish, she'd had a vision. The Island roads were an endless maze. There was no way out.

The awful truth is that, at an indeterminate point, the entire Island becomes one big cabin. The front door of this cabin is the loading door of whichever ferry is docked. There is no back door, though there is a trap door that opens up above the airport. Transportation to and from the Island being what it is, there are those days and nights deep in the secret season when, due to weather conditions, both the front and trap door are locked. The

Island roads, albeit primarily for vehicular traffic, are popular with the joggers, walkers and horseback riders.

standby line then, in high contrast to summer's carefree frisbee park, is a scene of dark mutterings and rueful sky-directed oaths. Perhaps most common, even for those with fifteen seasons worth of beach stickers, is "I swear I'm moving off this rock."

When the Island cabin doors are locked on a full moon, the package stores and self-help groups experience a surge, and the parking spots in the "wet" towns take on a healthy fullness. A sample snatch of bar conversation might begin "I'm thinking of a day trip to Boston."

Yes, this is a schizophrenic Island, with its manic and depressive seasons. But the ups and downs are the masks that hide the essential placidity of the place. There is a general unhurriedness that, as an Island driver, I can't help but attribute to an embargo on speed. The only place in our lives where rapidity is regulated is on the roads. Here on the Vineyard, the lower speed limits pace our lives and give us more time to appreciate the beauty that surrounds us.

Richard C. Skidmore is a freelance writer whose work has appeared in The New York Times *and the* Vineyard Gazette. *He has spent many of the last sixteen years living in Gay Head and driving on Vineyard roads.*

Bucolic Island scenes, such as this lily pond near Cranberry Acres, are in constant threat of being bulldozed under to make way for yet another housing development.

24

Conquest-Watching

BY ANNE W. SIMON

It is said that we are remaking the coastline, if not the entire continental U.S., in our own image. No one quite knows what our image will look like on the coast or how it will feel to live in such a place. Nor have we clearly defined the motive that drives us to this takeover of such a strong antagonist—nature in all its stubborn wildness.

The what and why may still be unknown but there is no question that we know how to do it. Extraordinary technological advance in this era endows us with the capacity to make what we want of nature. With enough cash or credit, a hamlet becomes a shopping center surrounded by a town on its way to being a high-rise city.

Conquest-watching could be a compelling tourist attraction, a newly-minted reason to come to Martha's Vineyard. On this little Island, a microcosm of the whole, man remakes nature—efficiently and mercilessly. Spend a few summers here and the fast alteration of this place will be unavoidable. Last year's quiet country road becomes this year's thoroughfare. No one person is responsible. Perhaps a land owner needs cash for totally understandable reasons, maybe sickness in the family or sending children to college. He sells to a developer who is in the quite acceptable building business. In the natural course of events, the developer files with the town planning board; abutters testify with violent objections, the board reasonably enough compromises, maybe cutting down the permissible number of units or demanding more open space, trying to keep a semblance of the old Island intact. The developer, with plenty of cash on hand, sues the town where coffers are slim. He can hold out; he wins. Now the road is a different place.

Multiply the one quiet road by ten and you get a bigger store, bigger highway to get to the store, a larger school, library, fire department, a crowded beach, a long line at the movies.

People used to come here because it was "unspoiled." The Island's natural resources supported some five or six thousand people, many birds, some undomesticated deer, skunks and other species. Fish and shellfish thrived in the clear, clean water, made a decent living for fishermen. Farming close to the warm Gulf stream produced plenty, life was secure. "We kept the Vineyard this way for 300 years" town fathers used to say "and

If a tree falls in the forest, does anyone hear!

there's no reason why we can't continue to do so.''

Today the human footprint is all over the place. The old salts and first families are only dimly evident, towns are run by business interests. It is a new fact of life that the old ways are over, here. No one even considers the possibility of keeping the Island as it was. Instead they debate the ideal rate of growth.

This is radical change. The motive behind its proponents and its opponents define the issues. Sometimes it is difficult to discover who's who. Some are unmistakable in their convictions. I guess I am one of these, making more noise than proper in the Hough-Thoreau tradition which I would like to be considered a part of, and, I am told by certain friends, becoming tediously predictable in pronouncements about the dangers of toxins in fish and such.

I know what my motives are. I trust the environment the way it was during my life and I want it to stay that way. For years I have studied and written about the alterations we make to the coast and ocean. The facts say we are endangering most species, including our own. I want that to stop. I want it in general, of course, but more directly for my grandchildren because their ability to survive is threatened, and I want them to live long healthy lives. Also selfishly, I want it for the Vineyard because this is the place in the world I know best and cherish the

Familiar Vineyard views will eventually look quite different if Anne Simon's prognostications prove accurate.

most and it is painful in the extreme to me to see it stagger and fall under the weight of man's intrusion.

These are the motives that make me talk and write so vehemently.

Growth addicts are harder to find. They are leaders in this six-town society, people whom you likely respect because of their work and position. They are big-shot contractors, selectmen, members of the Martha's Vineyard Commission, journalists. They profit by growth, one way or another. You might never know what lurks in their desk drawers. One person in a particularly responsible government job was recently found guilty in court of passing on insider real estate information to make a nice profit. Not long thereafter, the very same culprit presided at a public meeting concerned with planning. Nobody blinked.

The conquerors use land to make money. That is without doubt the prevailing motive. Eventually it will have to fail as the Island's limits are overrun. But short term, there is money to be made here by developing land. The first to sell were old-timers who inherited big family farms, had more land than money, and needed cash. The 1980's saw the bloom of the off-Island developer with money to invest, who heard there was good and notably unprotected land to be had on the Vineyard. By now, developers are selling to investors from Europe and Japan as well as land buyers and growth dealers all over the United States. Commerce flourishes in the towns which grow apace, and despite slumps in real estate—applauded by the nature protagonists—conquest proceeds.

I will chance a prediction of the Vineyard's near future. It will not be a Manhattan or Miami Beach due to fast erosion here and the distance from the mainland, but it will be crowded. The six towns, already stretching tentacles toward each other, will merge, becoming indistinguishable, one from the other. As beaches and dunes are removed by the rising sea, housing will move inland. People pressure will grow enough to threaten the water supply but even so, when there's no more space on the ground, there will be

building in the air. The local by-laws which prohibit high-rise appear no sturdier than the old-timers' conviction that they would keep the Vineyard as it had always been. Longer range, as what was is lost forever, so memories of its magic will fade and disappear, along with its putative protectors.

For once, I will be pleased to be found wrong.

Anne W. Simon is a writer on family matters and on the environment, particularly the coast and ocean. She has written for many periodicals and is the author of five books, most recently Neptune's Revenge: The Ocean of Tomorrow *and* The Thin Edge. *She lives in New York City, and summers at "Salt Meadow," her family compound in Menemsha. She is currently writing a book about older singles.*

Anne Simon testifies at the Kennedy Bill hearings at the Tisbury School in 1974.

The Edgartown waterfront along North Water Street, looking south toward the Yacht Club.

An Island from the Sea

BY WALTER CRONKITE

What first attracted me to the Vineyard was the sailing. I was cruising the area for the first time, and I dropped anchor in Edgartown and fell in love with it instantly, as I think everybody must.

There's a phrase that says, "If you see the Island at first from the water, you will fall in love with it." What the old saying means, obviously, is that the newcomer will fall in love with the Vineyard no matter how he sees it first. That certainly applies to me.

I was particularly amazed when I came back here the second time with my father, who was then in his early 80's. I sailed him into Edgartown. It was his first trip back to the East Coast from his mid-western domicile since World War I, and he casually said, "You know, I was actually here once. I was here with your grandfather, and we came into this very place. I remember it very well. We visited a relative of ours here. But I can't remember the name."

And as we walked down Water Street he kept saying "Now that looks like the house there" pointing to five or six different captain's houses along the waterfront. I thought to myself, that since our family never really had very much money, it was probably an early childhood illusion of his.

Six years later we decided to move to the Island, it was the place I wanted to be. When I first bought our house, after having vacationed on my boat a great deal, I went to one of the social functions in town. That evening, it seemed as though everyone already knew we had just moved in. Many people said things like "Oh, we're so *happy* you've decided to come to our little Island. We've been coming here for three generations, you know." It's always a put down for the newcomer. It happens to everybody it seems. Well, I got kind of tired of that boring repetition of the fact that I was new to the Island and that they weren't. After that summer passed and I got back to New York, I received a letter from a quite distant cousin from Rehobeth saying, "I'm so glad you decided to go back to the land of your ancestors." The letter went on to assert that we were directly related to the Norton family of Edgartown. And thus the house that my father seemed to remember was probably the old Captain Norton house. He turned out to be a cousin of my grandfather's, and a second or third generation Vineyarder himself. I was so happy to get back to the Island the following summer, because the first person who boasted of their Vineyard lineage could receive my retort that my family had been here for two hundred years. I'm proud to be, even if remotely, a Norton.

When I think back to when we first started coming to Edgartown, I'm amazed at how much it has changed. It is unfortunately no longer the little country village it once was. While I still love it and it still has most of its charm, it is now a resort and no longer a service community. Now you have to drive out to the Triangle to get to the stores to maintain sustenance. And the traffic in July and August now has become intolerable. But we have the advantage of being out from the middle of town, and it has now become my habit to take my boat to town when I have to go. I take my Whaler in and tie it up at the Yacht Club and go about doing my errands. It's much more delightful than going by car. I actually feel I'm making a little excursion. I sometimes imagine myself leaving the colony to sail to England for supplies.

Martha's Vineyard has become a won-

The Captain Norton House on North Water Street.

Some of Edgartown's more impressive boats line up for the annual coronation at the Yacht Club.

derful sailing base for me. Nantucket is too remote, although perhaps more dramatic. Any round trip from there to a mainland harbor involves a couple of days. But from the Vineyard I have a whole hemisphere of possible harbor destinations for a one or two day cruise. I can go out to Nantucket itself, or over to Cape Cod, or out into Buzzard's Bay or the Elizabeth Islands. There is a marvelous itinerary of places to explore on any given day. Also, it's quite picturesque sailing out of Edgartown Harbor and I can marvel at the beauty of our town at one end of the harbor—dressed in her sparkling white and serviceable, no-nonsense Yankee grays—and the wide expanse of Katama Bay at the other. We nearly always have strong southwesterly winds in the late afternoon, more consistently than on Long Island Sound where I sailed for many years before moving here.

The Edgartown Yacht Club is a key to my enjoyment of life on the Vineyard, and it serves several functions for Edgartown and therefore for me as a participant. First of all, it is an active yacht club. The Regatta is an important event each year. Then there is the sail training program and the weekly races are a major part of the waterfront activity of a waterfront town and therefore a major factor to the community. It is, as well, a social center for the Edgartown people, both the year-round residents and the seasonal members. And for sustaining the health of the harbor—in keeping down pollution and overuse, and all the other possible dangers that can occur at a resort rendezvous of this kind—the Yacht Club members are a focal point of concerned interest. And as a constituted body, outside of government, along with the Chamber of Commerce, the club is an important influence in the preservation and development of the harbor.

One of the reasons I cherish the Vineyard is that I am able to live a pretty isolated lifestyle at the house or on my boat, the Wyntje. Of course, at the beginning of each year we get the letters: "We're intending to be touring around in New England this coming summer, and just thought we might come to the Vineyard.

Two familiar Edgartown locales: the pond behind the Old Whaling Church and the Old Sculpin Gallery on Dock Street.

celebrity homes, á la Beverly Hills, but they don't get much of a shot at many of us because we're so far off the main roads.

One social aspect of the Vineyard that I find really special is that it is a wonderfully democratic society. Unfortunately there is a little separation between the so-called summer people and some of the year-round population. That is unfortunate, but probably understandable. But otherwise there really doesn't seem to be any sense of social stratification on the Vineyard at all. I think it's because we're all here for the same purpose. We are all geographically and physically a part of the same environment. I think it has to do with the nature of the residents of the Island as well. They've got a good, Yankee assessment of their fellow man, and it rarely is based on accomplishments in the outside world.

The Vineyard seems to me right on the edge of tipping over to the ruined side of the ledger in terms of overdevelopment. We're near the maximum that we can tolerate right now. There is no question that development—increased housing and some commercial expansion—is necessary, particularly to serve the year-round community. As population pressures increase here, as well as other special places in the country, we are simply going to have to make room for the greater demand. I think that can still be done, if it is done with intelligence. The growth must be controlled, especially from the standpoint of aesthetics and viability. We just don't have the facilities to take care of a lot more people. We've got problems of water supply, waste disposal, sewage, and transportation infrastructure. The Island has its limits by the very fact that it is an island and can not expand. Ideally, I'd like to see a larger winter time population and a growing off-season economic base, with less of a summer invasion. I'd like to see it even out a bit.

When I'm sailing I really leave the rest of the world behind. I don't even listen to the radio! When I get back to shore after a few days, I'm surprised at the state of the world sometimes. But on shore, it really isn't possible to live a reclusive life. Our home here is a fairly average household. We have our televisions and people are

Can you suggest a good place to stay?" Unfortunately, since my relatives usually take up most of our guest rooms during the summer, we just don't have room for the casual visitor. Sometimes, though, if we do have an overflow, I just stick them out on the Wyntje.

Despite a busy household, most people appreciate the fact that it is meant to be a retreat for all of us. There is something about the Vineyard apparently that impresses outsiders with the fact that all of us are here to live a relatively undisturbed existence, and they tend to respect that. I understand that taxi drivers do a tour of

tuning them in and out at all times of the day. And I get *The Boston Globe* and *The New York Times* in the morning. In fact, I probably absorb more news these days up here than in the city because I spend more time in the morning reading the paper.

I still have a hankering to be out there on the front line covering the major news events. That desire will never cease, I now know, but there does come a day when you realize it's time to enjoy the other things that life has to offer.

As I look out my window down to the harbor, the sun is casting a spectacle of light off the crisp blue water. I see a few whitecaps now, and the breeze is picking up from the southwest. I might as well scrap all plans for the rest of the day and head out to the Wyntje for a quick sail toward Vineyard Haven. We'll pack a little dinner and catch the sunset as it goes down behind West Chop. With a patchwork of clouds and a tartness to the air, it will be one of those special evenings when the dusk hues surround the boat, and I'm enveloped in a magical world of my own, where everything else seems happily irrelevant. And looking at the Island from the water, I'll fall in love with it all over again.

Since leaving the CBS Evening News *in 1982, Walter Cronkite has hosted various documentaries for CBS and PBS, and co-authored two books,* North By Northeast *and* South By Southeast, *with fellow Edgartownian, artist Ray Ellis. He is currently at work on an anxiously awaited autobiography and a third book with Ray Ellis about the West Coast. He is generally considered the most trusted man on Martha's Vineyard.*

Walter Cronkite in love with the Island and his boat, the Wyntje.

Robert Post and Sherman Goldstein, together again, surf fishing at the Gay Head Cliffs.

Fishing:
A Noble Avocation

BY ROBERT POST

While fishing at Gay Head, on a recent morning, I noticed a flock of starlings hung in the gathering light of a pale blue dawn. Thousands of birds folded and flowed as if giant hands were practicing origami with this feathered mass. I was there to fish for striped bass.

I still sleep uneasily with the memory of a large fish lost months ago. That fish was hooked as I languorously cast and retrieved an eel on the North Shore. It hit with the fury of a massive collision at home plate between Campanella and Mays.

I'm uneasy with the thought of its size. What unseen piscatorial forces could strip line effortlessly and break a wire leader as if it were crimped too hard between a pair of Herculean pliers? I still ache for that fish. But at the same time, I'm relieved I didn't have to decide to keep it or take it to the taxidermist— especially if it was over sixty pounds.

And it was a fifty-one pounder that Sherm Goldstein snatched from the undulating water, below the flowing waves of starlings, the previous morning. It was his accomplishment that drew me to the base of those majestic clay cliffs, with their sensuous colors and countless gullies, furrowed and eroded by the seasonal rains.

Sherm fishes hard. He also dresses like a male cardinal. His bright red slicker is a colorful advertisement marking his location. He likes to wear a woolen watch cap on cool fall nights. Festooned with entry buttons from past derbies, along with numerous fish pins awarded as prizes, the hat actually clatters when Sherm walks briskly along the beach. As he approaches, the buttons look like red, white, blue and yellow poker chips that were thrown at his head and haphazardly stuck to the side of his hat.

I share with Sherm more than friendship, which fishing has helped shape and strengthen. It is the compulsive drive to fish from the surf that binds us. Dawn and dusk, day after day throughout the Derby and into the late fall we are either fishing or thinking we should be fishing. We suffer joyously from fishing fever. Our malady is displayed on an old sign printed by Bickford and Carrier, Inc. of Greenfield, Massachusetts to promote the sale of their Anti-backlash Reel and Surf Rod Grips. Its multi-colored wording reads:

WARNING

FISHING POX
VERY CONTAGIOUS TO
ADULT MALES

Symptoms—Continual complaint as to need for fresh air, sunshine, and relaxation. Patient has blank expression, sometimes deaf to wife and kids. Has no taste for work of any kind. Frequent checking of tackle catalogues. Hangs out in sporting goods stores longer than usual. Secret night phone calls to fishing pals. Mumbles to self. Lies to everyone.

Our success catching fish may be a testimonial to our skill casting and the many hours, almost beyond reason, we devote to this sport—or what Peter Matthiessen calls "one of mankind's noblest avocations." But the bait we use,

Buddy Vanderhoop and Hollis Smith netting a good catch at the Herring Creek in Gay Head.

Growing up in Long Beach, New York, my only memory of herring was pickled and smothered with sour cream. My Grandma Sadie would proudly place it on the dinner table when I visited. I was amazed that the same grandmother who made chocolate chip cookies and peach pies could commit such an act of treachery. I never ate her pickled herring.

The herring industry on the Vineyard was thriving and prosperous in the late 1800's, although a conflict burdened the herring fishery at Mattakeset around 1868. The herring creek connects the fresh water of Edgartown Great Pond with the salty waters of Mattakeset Bay, now known as Katama Bay. In *The Story of Martha's Vineyard*, published in 1908, the fight between the farmers and the seiners was reported:

> "It seems that the farmers whose lands border the Great Pond, and are frequently overflowed by its high water, prefer an outlet across the beach direct to the salt sea that will keep the Pond drained to a level below their pastures. This, of course, makes the herring creek useless and starts a feud that only the courts can settle, for here the herring fishery proprietors were left with a dry and useless ditch to contemplate. . ."

including eels, bunker and herring also help with our success.

The richness of the Vineyard's sport fishing is not limited to striped bass, bluefish, bonito and false albacore. Also important are the smaller bait fish. For without the bait fish—those dark compact clouds containing hundreds of creatures that move as one—the bigger game fish, that have given the Vineyard an almost mystical reputation, would bypass the varied cobbled and sandy beaches.

Eels have an uncomplicated history as a bait used by surfcasters. Eel pots set in brackish ponds by old-timers like Captain Norman Benson never seemed to produce much hostility. I can remember many trips to Norman's back door where a dented squat washtub, covered with a cracked squalid looking tarp, sat in the shade, filled with the day's haul. After a few knocks on the door, Norman would come shuffling along ("Every man's grandfather") his deeply lined leathery skin a reminder of many days spent in a blistering sun tending his fish traps.

It's a little more complex with herring, however. A fine bait for the recreational angler, herring also have a long commercial history and an important place in Indian culture. I wasn't familiar with live herring until I moved to the Vineyard.

In addition to the seining nets, the capture of striped bass by the herring fishermen, whether intentional or not, probably occurred when the herring fishermen used a surf-net. As reported in the February 10, 1956, *Vineyard Gazette*, the surf-net "was a huge, hooped net with a handle several feet in length. When the herring school lay outside of the creeks, and could not readily be seined, men took these surf-nets and waded into the water, filling the net as full as they could handle it and then, with the handle or pole over a shoulder, they walked out to dump their flapping catch on the sand."

In the 1930's when the bass fishermen took their revenge, by cutting the seiners' nets, the herring were bringing a dollar a barrel for their scales alone. This could turn into a substantial sum of money since hundreds of barrels could be filled in a night. The scales were used to make an artificial pearl, called the Priscilla Pearl.

The Boston Post, May 22, 1923, ran the following story:

> Young boys equipped with long scaling knives strip each fish of the white, shiny scales which are then taken to huge vats and put through a refining process. Later, the substance is shipped in the form of lacquer to a factory at Hyannis where ropes of pearls are made that sell from five to three hundred dollars.
>
> R. H. Bodman and Eugene Dupee of Hyannis are the pearl kings who discovered the secret of making pearls from herring scales. Both are skilled chemists.
>
> During the war (WWI) there was a shortage of essence d'orient from Russia, which was used to transform glass beads into imitation pearls. It was then that Bodman and Dupee came to Martha's Vineyard and worked out their idea.

Between the farmers of the mid-1800's, the bass fishermen of the 1930's, and the fire that burned down the plastics factory where Ralph Bodman planned on converting fish scales to plastic, only the advent of WWII and the purchase of reprocessed herring by the War Foods Administration kept the herring industry going, until about 1954, when it died out.

The herring, the starlings, the stripers, the bluefish, all migrate with the seasons. The emotions they evoke can be seen in my wild determined look when news of the first bluefish blitz spreads in the fishing community. The blitz shatters the placid isolated solitude of the waters at Wasque Point with a dance for survival that jitter-bugs around the perimeter of the Island.

A call to Sherm creates more turmoil. Dropping the interests and immediate needs of our families, we will set out together, seeking bent poles and tight lines. History and tradition stalk the surf zone. Game fish, bait fish, and fishermen all soon will meet. There is passion in this

A sign in the window of a Menemsha fishing shack.

meeting of fish and fishermen. And this passion seems as natural as first love—natural, yet mysterious in unworldly ways.

Robert Post is the author of the highly acclaimed anthology of local fishing tales, Reading The Water *(The Globe Pequot Press, 1988). He considers himself a "fisherman trapped inside the body of a dentist." Post moved to the Vineyard in 1972, where he was introduced to surf fishing. Fourteen years later he won the Shore Division of the Martha's Vineyard Striped Bass and Bluefish Derby with an 18.95-pound bluefish. Since then he has won respect and credibility in the fishing community on the Vineyard.*

Action during the annual striped bass and bluefish derby at West Basin.

Remnants of another era at the Whiting Farm in West Tisbury.

This Side of the Brook

BY DIONIS COFFIN RIGGS

In the early part of this century the Mill Pond and its outlet into Tisbury Great Pond separated the town of West Tisbury into two distinct parts. We went "over the brook" to church, to school and to Mayhew's Store. The post office and Gifford's Store were on our side.

It's Saturday, and I'm out of school. School isn't too bad this year now that my sister Mary is a teacher. She graduated from Bridgewater in June, and this is her first school. She says I have to call her "Miss Coffin" in school. My mother and the other big sisters get here from New York only for their vacations. I live with Grandma, Grandpa, and Aunt.

William Baxter dropped in this morning on his way home from Aunt Mathilda's. She is Grandpa's sister and the widow of a sea captain. She lives on Old Country Road, so Mr. Baxter takes a short cut through the field opposite our house when he goes to take care of her horse and cow. He often stops in on his way home. He never stays long. He opens the door and runs without holding on to the door knob the way some people do. He told Grandma that Gifford's Store was out of molasses, and he didn't want to go over the brook to Mayhew's. Grandma said she had plenty, and she'd lend him some for his pancakes.

"I had my breakfast long ago," he said, "and Gifford says there's a barrel of molasses down on the wharf, and he's going to Vineyard Haven for it this afternoon."

"There's always something on the wharf," Aunt said.

"Well anyway, Em's probably going to the other store on her bicycle," Mr. Baxter said. "She likes to ride the thing."

Emily is his wife, and we see her riding up and down New Lane. Her hair is cut short, like a man's. It looks ridiculous, but Aunt says she is an artist and they are different. I like her paintings. One of them has two squirrels running up a tree. They look so real I love to watch them every time Aunt sends me there with a piece of cake or pie. Emily is the younger sister of George Manter, the farmer who lives down on the Neck. He has boats on Town Cove, and he lets us borrow his rowboat whenever we want to go to the beach to dig clams. Grandma says he is the kindest man in the world, always helping people.

When Mr. Baxter left I went with Aunt to the post office to mail her letters. Every week she writes to Aunt Etta who lives in California. Both Aunt Alvida and Aunt Henrietta were born in South American ports while Grandpa was whaling in the Pacific. They were little girls on shipboard and the sailors used to play with them. My mother was born here, right in this house.

Grandpa's younger brother, my great-uncle Dan, went to sea for one voyage, but decided he'd rather be a doctor than a sea captain. When he came home he "read medicine" with Dr. Luce before going to college. Dr. Luce had an office in his house two doors from Gifford's Store. Now his nephew, George Hunt Luce, uses it for a milk room. George Hunt has cows that graze in the pasture between

Aerial view of the small barrier between the West Tisbury Great Pond and the Atlantic Ocean.

a nickel apiece for leaches because he used them to bleed his patients.

Phoebe Cleveland, post mistress, took the letters. "You're late, Alvida," she said. "You usually get your letters here by Friday noon. It takes almost a week, you know, for your sister in California to get it."

On the way back we stopped at Capt. Luce's. He's not related to the doctor, unless they have the same ancestor way back. His house is nearly opposite ours and we can hear him when he swears at his horse. "Luce swears all the time," Grandpa says, "How can he run a good ship if he has to swear at his sailors?"

Capt. Luce's wife, Betsy, is a great gardener, always working in the little patch she has fenced in with chicken wire. She crawls under the wire and works on her hands and knees. If she has too many plants she throws them across the road and they grow there. Those were her plantain lilies that bloomed across the road this summer. The box bushes in front are all overgrown. Grandma calls her front yard "Betsy's jungle," but nobody uses the front door. In spring wisteria blooms over the back porch. Their daughter Susie is blind, so Aunt goes to read to her every once in a while. Grandma was making pies early Monday morning so Betsy got her washing done before Grandma did. They make a game of who's going to get her clothes on the line first each week. Grandma likes a west wind so they dry fast and smell good.

Today is cool and the trees are turning. Grandpa will harness Mack to the truck-wagon and go to his wood-lot down Tiah's Cove Road. I hope he takes me with him. Spark will go, of course, barking and chasing birds all the time. Mack seems to like his company. Grandpa has already cut down some of the trees. We will need a lot of wood for all the stoves, the kitchen stove for cooking and the others to keep warm—parlor, dining-room, and Miss Magay has a stove upstairs. She is the teacher of the higher grades, and she boards with us this year. She is very nice, and is trying to teach me French.

Grandpa is always talking sea-talk, but

New Lane and the Stepping Stones. When I want to go wading I wish those cows weren't there. Grandpa had a cranberry bog when he first came home from sea. He had big stones put in the stream that runs from the Mill Pond to Town Cove. That was how he crossed the brook to go to his bog from his house without going around the road. One trouble with wading at the Stepping Stones—you get leaches on your feet and legs. My mother didn't mind leaches when she was my age because her "Uncle Doctor Dan" gave her you usually know what he means. Sunday when we were driving up to church he let Mary drive. When he saw the Whitings coming down the hill he hollered, "Stand a-back, let that craft cut across your bow." So they got to the church ahead of us. Mr. Adadourian is the minister. He travels around a lot and tells us about the world. He brought Aunt some embroidery from Constantinople. Mr. Moody preaches when Mr. Adadourian is away. The two big Moody boys, Willis and Walter, work in Mayhew's store.

Grandma and Grandpa thought one church service on Sunday was enough, but Aunt goes across the road to the Baptist Church occasionally. One quiet afternoon she heard Grandpa's sea-captain voice as he came in from the barn, "Here's the milk, Mary."

I went with Aunt to the Baptist Church one time. Bill Hubbard is deacon, so he sat up front. He was on the lookout for the woodpecker that tapped on the side of the building for insects. His best shoes squeaked as he went down the aisle to scare it away. We heard him clap his hands and say, "Shoo! Shoo!" then squeak back up the aisle.

The Baptist Church is new. There was trouble in the Middletown Baptist Church when one member accused another of stealing her flatiron and people took sides. So they started to raise money for another church and got land across the road from Grandpa's house. There was a marvelous catch of fish in Deep Bottom Cove, fish that came in to spawn when the beach was opened. The Baptists sold enough fish to build a new church.

Each spring the beach is opened with horses or oxen and men with just hoes. They cut a channel from the Pond to the sea and the tide rushes through and makes it wider. Sometimes a storm closes it and they have to open it two or three times each year or the Pond would get too full. In the summer Grandma has a picnic at Quansoo when they open the beach.

Grace, my friend, and I often walk to Tiah's Cove on Saturdays. There is a swing hung from a tall oak tree in the yard where Nancy Luce, the poet, used to

Taken around 1914, this photograph shows Dionis Coffin Riggs's sister (far left) and others dressed in historical Indian regalia. During the years before World War I, an annual pagent took place in West Tisbury to recreate how Martha's Vineyard was first settled.

This well, across from the West Tisbury police station, dates back to the turn of the century.

The Athearn home.

Dawn comes to the Mill Pond in West Tisbury.

live. Grace's family live over the brook and they go to Lobsterville as soon as school closes because her father is a lobster fisherman.

The Looks live farther down New Lane. They call the place Crow Hollow. Uncle Allen Look is married to Aunt Eliza, Grandpa's sister, and they have four sons. Grandpa goes to see his sisters, either Eliza or Mathilda, almost every Sunday afternoon and takes me, too. I like to go to Aunt Eliza's best. We sit out on the veranda that looks over Uncle Ben's Hollow, and she brings out cookies. All the men are often there, too. Uncle Allen considers himself a farmer as many West Tisbury men do. Nearly every place has a garden where people grow their own vegetables. They usually have a horse and cow, always chickens, and perhaps a

flock of sheep. Only one of the Look sons is a farmer. Freeman Allen built a house next door to his parents, and took over the big barn across the road. He has wonderful big horses that he is very proud of. He rode one of his horses in the pageant. That pageant was a lot of fun. It told the history of the Island with Gosnold coming in on Luce's Pond and the Indians coming down a path through the woods. My sister Mary was an Indian maiden, and I was an Indian too.

James Look does do some farming. He built a house not very far from his old home and he has some geese, but he spends a good bit of time in Menemsha, fishing. He has an automobile, the only person around here who has. It seems funny to see it going up the Lane without any horse.

Capt. Slocum bought the old house across the valley from ours. He has put a funny roof on it to make it look like a house he had seen somewhere on the other side of the Pacific. He often comes to see Grandpa and once he brought me a big shell from some foreign place. He is the one who sailed around the world alone in the Sloop Spray and wrote a book about it.

Capt. Slocum tried growing hops. He plowed up the hollow across the road, and stuck in a lot of poles for the hops to grow on. But he left to go to sea again, and never came back.

I have to spend a lot of time at school. I go early in the morning, right after breakfast. My sister goes even earlier because she's the teacher. One or two of the Giffords—Flavel, Beatrice, Gordon, or Willis—and some of Henry Lyman Luce's children, join me for the half-mile walk. We stop at the Mill Pond to throw sticks in the falls and see them come out the other side, under the road. Eliashib Athearn lives in the little house with the well out front where he draws all his fresh water. He has an apple tree with apples that have seeds that rattle. He takes them from his pocket when we go by, rattles them against our ears then gives them to us. We go to the same school where my mother went. It's called "The Academy." It was a boys' school, but all the town children went there. We march in to piano music when the bell rings. School is boring, even with my sister teaching, except I always like geography, finding places like Kamchatka and the Fiji Islands that Grandpa talks about.

Recess is fun. We play London's Bridge is Falling Down, and Drop the Handkerchief. Sometimes the girls take each other's arms and walk around, around the circular concrete walk. The boys usually play baseball. When Lillian Davis came to this Island to live she played with the boys. She used to live on Nomans Land when her father was caretaker of that whole island. Nobody else was there in the winter. She had only her brothers to play with.

We walk back every noon for dinner. We often go over Brandy Brow. It's called that because there was a tavern on the hill at one time. You can still see the ruins where it burned down. After dinner we took a short cut (it's really longer) around the factory that used to be an old mill. Later it was the factory where a cloth called satinet was made. Emily Baxter used to work there and several other people too. My great-grandfather bought it when he broke his leg and couldn't go back to sea. The cloth was so good that when a man had a suit made of it he never needed another.

The afternoon at school seems long. It seems as if the hands on the Town Clock will never get to four, when we can go home. We watch it from our seats. Finally it strikes four chimes. Spark will be waiting for me at the gate. He'll bark, then run and jump up on me, eager for our after school walk, maybe as far as Tiah's Cove, if it isn't too dark.

I had to stay after school a few nights ago because I threw a note across the aisle to Bert. It was so late that Barty Mayhew was there at the post office with the stage, so I waited for the mail. Barty meets the boat in Oak Bluffs every morning and evening. When he drove up to the post office this evening he had a big bag that he handed over to Phoebe. She takes her time sorting it. That's why she's always the first to know what's going on in the world—in the town even.

Beach grass at Long Point.

"There's a letter from New York, Dionis," she said. "It must be from your mother." And it was. Packages came in later, and there was a package for me, too. I opened it right there. My big sister, Hannah, who is a nurse, had sent me a stockingcap, red with a long tassel. It will be nice to wear in the winter, but I wish I didn't have to wear long drawers. As soon as Barty gets the evening mail from Phoebe he goes with it to Chilmark. In the morning he goes through Middletown and stops at his old family place to change horses while Lillian Adams is sorting mail at the post office across the road.

"You're late, little girl," Aunt said. "It's about time to light the lamps."

Aunt watches the sunset each evening and notices when the lights come on. We have a shelf of kerosene lamps that she keeps clean and filled, with the wicks trimmed. Almon Tilton's light is usually first because his kitchen faces in our direction, then Mayhew's store, the blacksmith's, then all the other houses. When Antone Alley's comes on she says, "I guess it's time to light *our* lamps."

Dionis Coffin Riggs, Martha's Vineyard's most prolific poet, was born in Edgartown in 1898. She spent her childhood in West Tisbury with her grandparents who are the main characters in her best-selling book, From Off Island *(McGraw Hill, 1940). She now lives in the old family house in West Tisbury. Her books of poetry include:* Martha's Vineyard, Seaborn Island, *and recent booklets,* From The Vineyard *and* Far Places.

At dusk the oil lamps are lit.

Dionis Coffin Riggs, 92 years young, hugs three generations of offspring: daughter (right), granddaughter (left), and great-granddaughter.

Sunshine daydreams.

Quitsa Pond at dusk.

I Look for the Vineyard Everywhere

BY LISA GRUNWALD

I look for the Vineyard everywhere.

My husband and I had a farmhouse in New Hampshire last summer for a week. Nice place, very old and pretty, on a pond that was filled with fish. There were woods to explore. A stream. A view. I hated the place. The place was a swamp.

Morosely, I watched the sun set each evening, thinking about the Vineyard as if the Vineyard was a lost romance. This happens to me all the time. On the least traveled beach in the world, I'll decide that the sand is the wrong color, the waves don't catch the right light, the palm trees look ridiculous.

In New Hampshire, I tried hard not to give in. I didn't *say* the word Vineyard. I didn't want to be spoiled, or nostalgic. I didn't want to be unadventurous.

On the fourth day, my husband woke me at dawn. He wanted to go to the Vineyard, he said. He asked me if that was all right. I cried.

We cleaned the house all morning and gathered our things in the afternoon, and then we set out giddily for Woods Hole, like school kids cutting class. We giggled on the ferry, and then got quiet as the harbor appeared.

We reached the house just at sunset. Of course. Stood on the jetty side by side, closing our eyes against the light and the clean salt breeze and the limitless joy of arriving home.

Lisa Grunwald was born and raised in New York City and spends summers with her family at their home on Vineyard Sound in Tisbury. She has worked as a reporter for the Vineyard Gazette, *published a novel,* Summer *(Alfred A. Knopf), and is now an editor at* Esquire.

47

Reflections of another era.

First Impressions

BY JAMES HART

Someone back in landlocked Albany said, "Go to Martha's Vineyard, you'll love it, it's so beautiful."

I stood in the parking lot at Wood's Hole surprised by its vast macadam expanse, as though the shopping mall that was attached to it had fallen into the sea, that there was a Macy's and Sears laying sunken somewhere beyond the bulkhead.

And then the large clunker of a boat came into view, followed by a collection of birds, not dissimilar to ones I had observed behind dirty tug boats on the Hudson.

Outside the terminal building couples held hands and cuddled close to one another. The fall breeze seemed to push them even closer together. As I stood on the deck of the ferry I felt I was entirely alone. It was a strange solitary state, one that almost heard a trumpet behind it, with a strange male voice in the background, the kind that used to introduce newsreels in the thirties, shouting something like, "Man of Destiny takes wrong boat, Tragedy."

I found the snack bar immediately and bought two beers. I didn't want to have to wait in line with all those ridiculous couples. My trip across the bay was lost in deep sighs and confusion, a reaction to considering what was happening in my life. I was beginning the painful process of separation and divorce. As this floating Greyhound bus reached the dock, I realized that I was going to need a few more cocktails to get me through the day.

I envisioned a dark wood, rum soaked cellar or a breezy, white ducked, waterfront club. I was directed to a bar in Oak Bluffs. The name I thought, suggested something in the latter style.

There was nothing elegant here. It reminded me of many of the bars which dotted the Hoosac Valley. This bar though lacked the lingering odor of wood smoke and was without the mandatory pickled eggs and pigs feet. Otherwise it seemed a copy. There were toothless old men and hairy babies and every imaginable form of domestic crisis on display. In addition there was a special form of disdain for me, the lowlander at the end of the bar. I sat there for hours trying to strike up some sort of conversation with someone. It was not possible. At some point I walked across the street for a bowl of clam chowder. Its quality didn't seem very different than that offered at a bar very near Troy, New York.

Late in the afternoon I left my stool bundled against the cold fall day and walked back to the ferry in Vineyard Haven.

Somehow I hadn't gotten it, there was no charm for me here. I walked down the long road by the water. I was once again overtaken by my own thoughts about what waited for me on the other side. Not even a full afternoon of beer swilling could interrupt these obsessions.

Then in front of me was the ultimate symbol of my journey, the landmark that would stick in my mind, and every time Martha's Vineyard was mentioned I would smile to myself, as rows and rows of cylindrical gas and oil tanks would pop into my vision. It was hard for me to comprehend but there it was, there was my romantic landscape by the sea, Oil City.

How could the people who lived here not understand? How could the couples so intricately connected not react? How could it be that I was the only one who saw them?

On the other side of the Island from the gas tanks are the simple pleasures of Menemsha.

As the ferry sailed across to Wood's Hole I could watch nothing else. I was mesmerized by the tank's shape and color.

The sight altered and galvanized my memory. Shortly after returning home I completely forgot that I had ever been there. People over the years would mention the Vineyard, and through some strange mental trick no doubt caused by the searing sight of those strange tanks along the harbor, I would respond as though I had never visited, as if someday I would have to check it out.

About ten years elapsed and on a late spring day I met a woman on a train. We both had gotten aboard at Hudson, New York, and were headed into Manhattan. We had one of those unique conversations, the kind that makes you think that Amtrak plots romance as a secret tax supported government service.

In no time we were dating and she invited me up to her place on the Vineyard to spend a weekend. I was anxious to make this trip, mainly to see if this Manhattan romance would survive a little salt air and secondly because I thought I had never been to the Vineyard.

I flew in from New York on a beautiful crisp June day and was met by the long legs and wide smile that told me instantly that this was to be more than a brief affair, there seemed something permanent about us before we even knew it, and her smile that day was a clear signal that we were going to at least survive the greeting.

She drove me to a strange sounding place named Menemsha in order to see the sunset. I thought she was pushing the scenery a bit. I mean, from the plane to the sunset seemed a bit excessive to me, but she insisted. The sun was beginning to set in wild pastel shades over the water. We shared a clam chowder from a little seaside stand, and we allowed the beauty of the setting sun to move our bodies a bit closer together.

I said something sophomoric like "This is the most beautiful place I have ever seen." After sharing this affirmation of her taste she moved yet a little closer. I had clearly passed one of her first tests, appreciating a Menemsha sunset.

That night was champagne, lobster and a long walk along a dark beach, a tour of fishing boats and moonlight through our first shared window by the sea. Something happened here, I couldn't tell if it was just the siren's call or the setting sun or middle age or finally finding, "the slow black, slow crow black, fishing boat bobbing sea," or the woman to drown for, or if I had just had a long flight and a sudden romance.

A short six months later, friends of mine were flying to the Vineyard for my wedding. This woman and I had decided to get married, and for our first year together we decided to do it on the Island. You can see the ambivalence that I have. Imagine an Island and a woman which combine and connect to seduce a guy who didn't even recall his first time there!

Probably a month or so later I was driving down Beach Road from Oak Bluffs to Vineyard Haven when the tanks on the right hand side loomed in front of me and broke open the memory of having been here so many years before. I found it hard to believe that I had made such a big deal about them, now they seemed to blend into the scenery, painted the right color and even the shapes seemed round and manageable.

I often wonder if other day trippers are ever affected by them in the same way that I was so long ago. Sometimes when I see a depressed and tired face on one of those tourists I want to tell them my story, or say, "Listen, if you really want to appreciate this place you'll have to go away for a little while and take a train ride."

James Hart is a writer of poetry and fiction. He is currently working on a novel. He lives with his wife Carly Simon in Tisbury and New York City.

Joel Zoss in a double exposure off Gay Head. This portrait was originally taken for an album cover but was ultimately rejected on the grounds that it might have religious implications.

A Floating World

BY JOEL ZOSS

I don't want to talk about how much the Vineyard has changed. In some ways it's changed beyond recognition, but I've changed too and I'm in no position to determine whether the changes I've seen are good or bad. Consequently I'm going to talk about parts that don't change because they're memories.

When I was a boy living in Menemsha I used to talk to old sea captains about sailing ships and ghosts. I was awed by the diversity of forms to be found washed up at the water's edge. As I grew older my explorations expanded, and my returns to the Island became pilgrimages. In Chilmark an old salt taught me how to dowse for water and expounded on electricity in the body in a way I did not hear again until I encountered the Hindu chakras. It was always on the Vineyard that my understanding of the luminous nature of existence flowered. I have often heard visitors say that they think the Vineyard is a place where the boundaries that separate realities are thin; for me everything on the Island is alive and teeming, like a scene in one of those medieval paintings that shows demons below the ground and angels in the trees.

A few years ago a Native American shaman visited me in Chilmark. He said that he liked the Vineyard but found it a bit stifling, and when I pressed him he said that what he meant was that the Vineyard was infested with dead spirits. He said most of them were sailors, and he asked me if eccentricity and drinking problems were common among the Islanders. I told him that I had always understood that they were; he explained that this was so because some deceased sailors had continued to satisfy their appetites through living bodies by taking possession of people who were open to them through disease or confusion. He explained that many men had died violent deaths in the old sailing days. Malnutrition, alcoholism and loneliness were constant companions on voyages that lasted for years, and many of the sailors who died at sea were extremely disoriented when they left this sphere. Obviously it took a certain type of person to sail into the unknown in the first place. Anyway, such deaths presented optimal conditions for the creation of ghosts, and when sailors became ghosts they returned to their home ports.

My guest's analysis made a lot of sense to me at the time, particularly because a few years earlier I had participated in a spontaneous exorcism involving one of the Island legends I had heard as a boy. In this story the sailor's ghost is not the mischievous one.

Near the spot where Peter took the photograph that goes with this article I was walking one day with the woman who ten years later became my wife. She and I had been walking on this beach long enough to attain that state of ecstasy familiar to those who walk upon Gay Head beaches when we came upon a place where a great fire was burning unattended. We lingered for a while, then turned up a dirt road to find our car. While we were walking through the weeds and mist I heard a sudden gasp and intake of breath, and before I could turn to see what had happened my companion was crying.

"Oh! She's so unhappy!" she said.

"Who?" I said.

"That poor woman," she replied. "Oh, she's so unhappy!"

I couldn't see anybody. Tears were streaming down her face. I realized she was seeing with her heart.

"Who?" I repeated.

"I don't know," she replied. "We have to help her! We have to help him too!"

"Who? How?" I said.

"I don't know," she replied. "She's dead, but she doesn't know it."

I realized we were not far from a house I had known as haunted all my life. No one ever lived there. Every few summers some enterprising college kids would clean it up and move in and then move out in a week. Island people would have nothing to do with this house. The landlord kept it just short of dereliction.

The story I had heard was that during the last century a sailor and his sweetheart had married and moved into the house. They lived there only a short time before he went to sea on a voyage of a couple of years. His boat went down in a storm and all hands were lost. His wife refused to believe he had died and spent the rest of her life faithfully keeping the house ready for his return. Then she continued waiting. Sometimes she was seen or heard going up and down the stairs, and sometimes she was seen on misty nights lighting a beacon or going down to the sea with a lantern to see if his boat was returning. Lots of people had seen her, especially men fishing for bass on the beach at night. I turned to my companion and asked her if the woman was carrying a lantern.

"She's not from this time," she replied. "Her dress is too old. She's going down to the water. Why doesn't she know she's dead? She's not supposed to be here."

"Not here?" I said.

"Yes," she said. "Dead people aren't supposed to be here. Something is keeping her here. Her desire. She died. Her love is keeping her here. She is very confused."

"Does she live in that house?" I asked.

"Yes! How did you know?" She was shaking now and tears were splashing down onto her sweater. I told her everything I knew about the legend.

"Yes, that's it!" she cried. "Help me! She won't believe he's dead because no news ever came back. He knows he's dead but he can't leave because her desire is keeping him here. Oh, this is hard!"

"Why don't you tell her he's dead?" I asked.

"She's gotten inside me but I don't know if it goes the other way."

"Try," I said.

The Vanderhoop Homestead near the Gay Head cliffs overlooks the shore and has long been associated with haunting tales.

Gay Head, foggy night.

She turned dark red and stood very still. "What a funny way they spoke! Listen! She understands me! She sees him!" Her tears stopped. She began breathing in and out very rapidly. I realized she had been concentrating so hard that she had stopped breathing. She reached for me and we almost fell over.

"Is it okay now?" I asked.

"Yes," she said. "They're gone. I know it. I showed her that her husband was dead. She believed me. She saw him. She went. Then he was free to go. They're gone."

"Will they ever come back?"

"No," she replied. "They're gone."

We continued down the road until we reached our car. The air had grown cooler. "Let's go to the Aquinnah Shop and get some pie."

Joel Zoss began his professional career as a songwriter and musician, whose well-known song "Too Long At The Fair" appeared on his album Joel Zoss *(Arista Records, 1976) and was successfully covered by Bonnie Raitt. While he still sings around New England, his main efforts are now literary. Among his publications are six books about baseball, including* Diamonds In The Rough *(Macmillan, 1989), a novel* Chronicle *(Simon & Schuster, 1980) and the reference work* Almanac Of The Vietnam War *(World Almanac, 1985). When he's not at his home in Leverett, Massachusetts he lives in a well-appointed tent compound in Chilmark with his wife and their children.*

During the late 70's and early 80's, John Belushi and his tightly knit coterie moved through the Vineyard social circuit like a pack of charismatic gypsies. He often showed up, incognito, to play drums at the Hot Tin Roof, and hang out at the Ocean Club at four corners in Tisbury.

Celebrity Status

BY JIB ELLIS

The Island of Martha's Vineyard has a reputation for beauty, serenity and coded glamour with the celebrity demographics of a Betty Ford Clinic without walls. Even though the terms of fame vary, the Vineyard is deluged with noted figures who come here for non-star status. The resort terrain, protected by a sizable moat and qualifying prices, boasts tracts of beach and antiquity while only murmuring about its legion of noted homeowners.

The Vineyard salad of famous names and faces has become a form of honorarium, a quiet announcement of success, combined with New England humility and anti-Palm Springs discretion. Wayne Newton doesn't live here. We don't have game show hosts, but we do have a heavy concentration of T.V. news, literary and artistic heavies. Neither Sonny, Cher, nor Yoko Ono care about Martha's Vineyard while William Styron, Walter Cronkite and Alfred Eisenstadt do. Martha's Vineyard is a veritable gotto (a ghetto for them that's got) for those who seek quiet taste in their triumphs.

The Island history dates back to Moshup, the Wampanoag tribal legend who rose from the sea to care for the original Vineyard settlers. The fishing tribe still flourishes on its own lands in Gay Head, but were nearly vanquished with the arrival of Anglican revision. Thomas Mayhew, Jr. came to the Vineyard from England in 1642 to settle in what is now Edgartown. That was all right with everyone, until his father, Thomas, Sr. arrived in 1646 to govern the initial white settlement and introduce the Wampanoags to things like Christianity and wing collars.

His grandson Experience Mayhew set about to cultivate the Island population followed by schoolmaster Nathan Mayhew. Mayhews still abound. Any Mayhew is an on-Island celebrity.

The Island definition of a celebrity is one with sufficient respect to forego judgmental scrutiny. He or she will personify positive image, trust and a neighborly Island belonging. The early Vineyard families, including the Mayhews, Manters, Whitings, Nortons and the Wampanoag community, all qualify as celebrities. They belong. They all merit a smile, unchallenged respect and check cashing privileges.

Martha's Vineyard guarantees its media celebrities, often with only a tax bracket in common, a particular non-fame, an unassuming anonymity they cannot enjoy elsewhere. For instance, Jacqueline Bouvier Kennedy Onassis can shop without being swarmed, at least by Vineyarders, and Islanders won't tell tourists where she lives. When John Hersey picks up his *New York Times*, he waits in line, perhaps behind Art Buchwald or Katharine Graham buying *Washington Posts*. When author Marianne Wiggins was married to and living with Salman Rushdie, and was fleeing the Ayatollah's wrath, there were rumors that she was back on the Island, but no one discussed her. If she were here to hide, which it turns out she wasn't, the Islanders didn't want to interfere. She, after all, had been one of us. Our celebrity encampment enables these subjects of mass fantasy to live in a scenic neutral zone, undaunted by papparazi.

The Vineyard is much more faded cedar

Carly Simon and Jacqueline Onassis at a booksigning party for Amy the Dancing Bear *at the Bunch of Grapes, in Tisbury.*

Marianne Wiggins, before moving overseas and marrying Salman Rushdie, lived in Chilmark for a few years in the late 70's where she wrote novels, and an essay for On the Vineyard, I.

shingle than glitz, but when a near-glitz celebrity buys a home here, they can still fit the meld. We tend to reappraise their image, by virtue of wanting to live on the Vineyard, and link them with our truth mongers and naturalists. A decade ago, Dan Aykroyd and John Belushi both bought Chilmark homes. We already trusted Carly Simon, James Taylor and Christopher Reeve, so we embraced the Saturday Nighters for choosing our ancient ways. They were included in the Island and by unwritten proclamation, left alone. When the curious asked where they lived, directions would be offered to the nearest landfill.

After all, the celebs make up a great portion of our tourist appeal—even New Jersey has beaches—and no one really wants to scare the notables off. When the lime-green-acrylic-pant-suited masses, filled with eager curiosity and toting instamatics step off the ferry, they expect to see Patricia Neal fishing from the Chappaquiddick bridge with James Taylor and Mia Farrow. Alas, Mia doesn't live here anymore, Patricia Neal may play croquet but doesn't fish and the Taylors all stay up-Island.

The Vineyard is not media heaven like Beverly Hills, where the phone book reads like T.V. Guide. Our phone book reads more like Who's Quietly Who, but the stars are definitely not shut-ins. Carly Simon is often visible, casually shopping on Vineyard streets, Michael J. Fox married Tracy Pollan, who's family summers in Gay Head, and Bill and Rose Styron may have coffee at a Tisbury bakery. Our noted names don't need disguises, there are no celebrity house tours, the stars are already quite visible.

In fact one of the summer big events is the celebrity auction, with chances for appreciative aspiring celebs to buy a sailing trip with Walter Cronkite, a tour of "60 MINUTES" with Mike Wallace and in 1988, a live performance by Carly Simon in the high bidder's home.

Art Buchwald is the annual auctioneer, and the cause is Martha's Vineyard Community Services, an Island multiple, United Way-esque organization with services from daycare to counseling.

When auctioneer Buchwald put Carly's housecall on the block the bidding was furious, but finally reduced to a pair of avid, wealthy enthusiasts. One topped $20,000, the other went to $22,000, Mr. Buchwald was frothing, Carly was beaming, the crowd was intense and Community Services saw funding hope grow for the year.

The two bidders were not about to relent, so Carly came up with a biblical compromise. She would sing in both homes, the men would pay $26,000 each, and everyone would be happy: Community Services, the winning bid families and perhaps, most of all, the crowd at peak frenzy, who were watching money, power and goodwill all holding hands beneath the active Buchwald gavel. The biggies annually give their presence for good causes.

Famous residents are our only recharging natural resource, but sundry groups have different stars, so the Vineyard sports success in varied fields. James Cagney, Katherine Cornell, Lillian Hellman and Ruth Gordon all lived here but so do an elite league of academics. Robert McNamara lived here. Three former presidents of Yale: A. Bartlett Giamotti, Kingman Brewster and A. Whitney Griswold all had Vineyard homes. Thomas Mendenhall, retired president of Smith, and Jerome Weisner of MIT live on the Island within minutes of diva Beverly Sills, cellist Yo Yo Ma, and economist Lester Thurow.

Residents of assorted fame and ranges of success, traverse the moat of emotional safety to wear flannel shirts and drive the vehicles they all wish they had at age 15. The Vineyard is for everyone a means of auditing life, not taking it for credit, but it is a vast green room to those of imposing fame. Even those of more subtle fame enjoy bucolic Island solace. Julian Hill, a long time summer resident of West Tisbury invented nylon for DuPont 50 years ago and his wife Polly, a longer term summer resident, is a world renowned horticulturist. Anthony Lewis of *The New York Times*, noted historian David

Dan Aykroyd, originally a member of the Belushi contingent, still owns a home in Chilmark and shows up occasionally.

Victor Pisano and Richard Dreyfuss at the annual Nathan Mayhew fundraiser.

59

Historian David McCullough lives in West Tisbury and enjoys frequent visits from family members. He hosts his own PBS television program which is periodically taped from his home.

Alan Dershowitz with his wife Carolyn Cohen. He takes time off from his frequent T.V. talk show schedule, teaching commitments and legal responsibilities to retreat to Chilmark obscurity.

Peter Greenough and Beverly Sills have a busy social schedule during the summer.

McCullough, and cartoonist/writer Jules Feiffer all live in West Tisbury, while cartoonist/writer Shel Silverstein lives in Oak Bluffs, as does television writer Marty Nadler, who owns "the house that Laverne and Shirley built." Legal mogul Alan Dershowitz, whose clients range from Claus Von Bulow to Leona Helmsley, spends July nestled with his new wife and child on Middle Road in Chilmark, and is often seen riding the waves at Lucy Vincent.

In a different camp, Ernie Boch, who must be a hero to a nation of automobile dealers, has a vast home in Edgartown. Retired dean of the National Cathedral and grandson of Woodrow Wilson, Francis B. Sayre, lives in the Yankee-swanky, brisk swim and sensible shoes West Chop area of Vineyard Haven. Artist Tom Maley is in West Tisbury and Gay Head is teeming with successful psychiatrists each summer. Terry Melcher, Beach Boys writer and producer, and son of Doris Day, also summers in Gay Head. Pharmaceutical product heir Farleigh Dickinson, lives in Edgartown, near the heirs to the first printed American railroad schedule fortune. Fame of every sort is represented.

Many of the off-spring and siblings of Island celebrities comprise a broad alternative population of over-educated builders and craftspeople and a large post-hippie/beatnik segment. They grow and eat vegetables, have already tired of making their own yogurt and now roll their own oats. They name their children Sky and Sparrow instead of Jason and Jennifer and play dulcimers instead of golf, but they are often able to do so because someone in the family was a celeb. The downwardly mobile league may have moved to the Island after summering here with parents and grandparents, and settled into alternative Island living. They play down their fame and names, but often cannot deny aristocratic cheekbones, inheritance and forms of social celebrity.

Then, of course, there are all those Mayhews, Nortons and Whitings. There are the swordfishing Pooles, the seafaring Vanderhoops, the football Araujos and the ketchup Heinzes. Celebrity on the

The Vineyard's relaxed lifestyle allows for the semblance of a "normal" life for some of the country's most noteworthy personalities.

Vineyard is not a prerequisite, but an acquired non-status. Celebrity is really only membership, and it takes good spirit and manners to belong.

Jib Ellis, former reporter at large for The Martha's Vineyard Times, *is a freelance writer who lives with his wife Jean in Oak Bluffs. He was a regular columnist for* The Boston Herald American, *and* Boston Magazine, *as well as the New England correspondent for* Advertising Age. *He is currently at work on a novel.*

Jib Ellis and Patricia Neal at the annual croquet tournament fundraiser at the Point Way Inn in Edgartown.

The Brookside Farm on Middle Road in Chilmark is transformed into a winter wonderland during a gentle weekend snowfall.

Snow Walk

BY PHYLLIS MÉRAS

Had I a choice of Island seasons nowadays, mine would be winter—winter when the woods are white and stone walls arch like dragon's backbones above the fields. I am describing a snowy winter, of course, that sculpts the landscape into new shapes so that, now and again, even on roads that I know well, I find that I have made the wrong turn and am adventuring down some new path to a strange house that I have never seen before.

At Sweetened Water Farm that happened this last winter, after I had passed the horses dressed against the cold in their green blankets and had started down a road into the woods. In the dark and snow, I lost my way, and never found the house that I was seeking, but I did happen on new ones and on meadows that were a surprise to me.

There is always adventure to an exploration on the Vineyard in a snowy winter, by car or on foot. Sometimes, I am up early enough so that bird and animal tracks are still the only marks in the snow—rabbit paw prints, deer hoof tracks. I am forever peering at the snow to see who has disturbed its loveliness before I do with my big red rubber Polish boots. When I am woods walking in winter, I prefer being alone—except for the animals and the birds, but I am always grateful for their company, even if it comes only from feeling a buck's presence from his hoof prints, or simply hearing woodpeckers tapping.

When I walk an Island beach in winter, similarly, the enjoyment is the greatest when I am alone with the black ducks and the gulls—when the beach and its driftwood treasures are all mine.

When I was a child, I dreamed of being an explorer, and on an untouched winter beach I can believe sometimes that I have

A snowfence protects the dunes in winter.

Summer memories drift into daydreams at the Whiting Farm, West Tisbury.

One of the seven wonders of the Vineyard—the rambling Oak Tree of North Tisbury.

A view of the Keith Farm from Middle Road.

Winter storage.

Tashmoo. This last year, I did not, though David Dandridge tells me there was fine skating on the Lagoon ice for the first time he can remember. My outdoor pursuit tended to be that simpler one of walking, of finding the huckleberry bushes as thick with snow blossoms as the shad is with its showy blossoms in the spring; of treading paths paved with frost diamonds, and looking in the Indian Hill woods for boulders turned into crouching toads of snow.

And what of Island winters when there is no snow?

Why then there are tawny fields to admire and elephant gray tree trunks faintly touched with pink; blue skies and red-gold sunrises and sunsets.

There are the brown and gold of fallen leaves and pine needles; green-red patches of sheep laurel; the deep dark green of Leonard Athearn's holly in West Tisbury, and the excitement of finding, on the coldest, blusteriest day, those tight curled leaf buds that give promise that spring comes.

Yes, of course, even I relish the sound of that first pinkletink and the sprouting of the earliest skunk cabbages. But spring brings people back to shores and fields and woods. On chilly winter days, in those Island places where I choose to roam, I often am the sole human invader.

Phyllis Méras is travel editor of The Providence Journal *and has written about travel for other newspapers, including* The New York Times. *She is the author of* Castles, Keeps, and Leprechauns *(Congdon & Weed) and eight other books. She has a home on Music Street in West Tisbury and is the contributing editor for the* Vineyard Gazette.

actually become one as I watch the green sea thrashing and the gulls diving over the ice-capped rocks. It is easy then to forget that, when summer comes, there will scarcely be sand to see for all the bathers sunning.

This past winter was, by my standards, an exceptionally fine one with its snow and the cold that kept the snow on the ground so long. Other years, the snow has seemed to go too soon. But this year, there was ice in Oak Bluffs harbor, on Sunset Lake, the Ice Pond, the Lagoon. All helped to give that sense of isolation that is what I long for in a Vineyard winter. Only in the winter, these days, can the Island be all mine. And it is then, too, that Oak Bluffs' gingerbread cottages are at their best with a touch of snowy frosting and Edgartown's black-shuttered captains' houses get an especially grand look. As for the Gay Head cliffs, they rise somehow more monumentally after a snow and Menemsha's shacks seem cozier.

Some winters, I have indulged in wintry pastimes—skating on ponds at Lambert's Cove, tobogganing at Lake

Sunday Pastime

BY RAM DASS

We were a delightful, rather geriatric crew that July in our rented house in Menemsha. It was one of those months for which the Vineyard is treasured, in which time is suspended, and life is marked off in fish chowder and key lime pies, naps in the sun, mystery stories, morning swims, wild roses and shell gathering expeditions.

Dad was in his mid-eighties and still enjoyed a good cigar, and each time he sat down in his deliberate fashion, he would mumble to himself, "There we are." Phyllis, my stepmother, in her sixties, was continually frustrated about an elusive word or other in the crossword puzzle, and won at Yatze more than a fair number of times. Her mother, Angela Hersey, who was pushing ninety, was a terrible flirt. She and I were sort of secretly engaged because I had given her a ring that somebody had left for me with a flower on the stage after a lecture. Besides that, I had "given away" Phyllis when she married Dad, which made me sort of Angela's, anyway. And as for me, I was spending the vacation with the family as "Richard," taking a break from being Ram Dass.

One Sunday, when my three nieces were visiting from the mainland, we decided to make a movie. Since my father's hobby had been making jelly and jam, we cast him as Bartholomew Gosnold, a distraught jelly maker in England who was running out of a rare type of grape needed for the jelly. The first scene was in the English kitchen where jelly production was underway. Dad, as Gosnold, was goading his scullery maids (my nieces, and Phyllis's mother, Angela) to stir the pots and work faster. He was to be grumpy.

This presented a problem for me as the director. In his earlier years, as President of the New Haven Railroad, there had been plenty of grump, but now he was continually sweet. So it took some goading, but finally he bravely swore and yelled at the girls, after which he mumbled softly to nobody in particular, "There we are."

Some rascally gypsies, played by Phyllis and me, (who were up to no good, though I can no longer recall what our nefarious objective was) lured Gosnold by means of a secret map, that was drawn on my bald head, into a boat trip (the rowboat was all we had) to a faraway Island where there was a reputed vineyard that produced the rare and precious grapes.

Since the rowboat leaked badly, we opted not to brave the deep, so we made ocean waves out of a heavy blue living room rug that we labored to bring out onto the grass and place under the boat. The ocean crossing was accompanied by a group rendition of "We sail the ocean blue, and our saucy ship's a beauty..." from *Pirates of Penzance*. Actually, all the scenes required the actors to burst into song at the least provocation. As the director, I thought these out-of-tune renditions gave the film a sort of "Kurt Weil flavor."

When we arrived on the Island we found that it was owned by Wise Rebecca (Angela) and her three Island beauties (my nieces, now transformed from scullery maids by the magic of sarongs). Angela, who idolized Ruth Gordon, was eager to embark upon her new career as an actress, but kept dozing off in the sun just when we needed her. I explained to her that as Wise Rebecca she was to start the scene by instructing the maidens about the facts of life. The camera rolled, I shouted

Ruth Gordon, one of the Island's all-time favorite personalities, in 1975.

The Vineyard's finest.

"Action," and she proceeded to tell them how to make a lemon meringue pie. In the midst of this initiation rite, the girls sighted the Gosnold boat coming, and they asked Wise Rebecca about "men." All she would say was that they were "trouble," and with an ingenuous look, reverted to her pie recipe.

After the landing, the greedy Gosnold found the Vineyard with the prized grapes and rubbed his hands gleefully. Then, bargaining for the Island began between the mean Gosnold and Wise Rebecca. Gosnold was now accompanied by his tipsy daughter, Martha, played by Phyllis, the only one of us with real acting experience. In true Stanislavsky style, she mixed herself a gin and tonic to prepare for the scene, which mercifully had to be cut short because we were running out of film. In the end Gosnold traded a tape recorder with a Chopin Nocturne playing on it for the Island, which he then presented to his daughter Martha.

The rest, of course, is history.

Beach grass silhouetted by the setting sun.

Ram Dass is the author of many books about spiritual growth and service, including Be Here Now, The Only Dance There Is, Grist For The Mill, Miracle Of Love *and* How Can I Help? *(with Paul Gorman). He tries to take some time from his busy lecture circuit to relax on the Vineyard each summer.*

Ram Dass meditating on the Vineyard Sound from his Menemsha perch during the summer of 1977.

Lambert's Cove Beach panorama.

Nudity sneaks onto the periphery.

Lambert's Cove

BY WARD JUST

Any beach has its cycles, good years and bad years like the cultural life of a nation. Ten years ago, Lambert's Cove, then as now, was a family beach and tolerant, up to a point. The northern part of the beach, near the Coca-Cola river, was often occupied by a few young women who preferred to sunbathe topless. They were discreet and usually covered themselves when standing or swimming. This was not voluptuous Lucy Vincent, after all, but decorous Lambert's Cove, unexciting as an old shoe.

There were not many topless and no one minded until one afternoon a burly tourist in a Wesleyan University T-shirt approached the young woman I was with and asked me if she could, uh, please cover herself—he and his wife were with their young children and it wasn't good for them, nudity, a public beach, etcetera.

I was startled. Nothing like that had ever happened before.

Well, I said, really, it was a large beach and this part of it had always been topless, if you wanted to be topless. It was like the smoking section of an airplane, ha ha.

He sighed, unconvinced. He kept his face averted from my topless friend, as if the sight of her would turn him to stone, or worse. And he seemed to think that I had the power to change my young friend's mind, a laughable notion.

Suddenly Wesleyan's wife, furious, exclaimed *Oh, Jesus Christ!* Another topless woman appeared, and another and another. Her family was surrounded by topless young women, many of them scarcely older than she was. These young women were like the Cossacks who appeared on horseback to harass Bonaparte's great army as it fled the suburbs of Moscow. *Oh Christ*, she said again, and gathered her husband and their young children—boys, as a matter of fact—and beat a retreat back up the dunes to the house they had rented. It was the last time, I think, since we never saw them again, either that summer or later.

But we wondered if we had won a Pyrrhic victory, and were about to enter a long Russian night. Were reactionary forces gathering themselves out there in Reagan's America?

No chance, happily. There was tranquility, or anyway monotony, for a few years, though each year there seemed to be fewer topless. My wife and I began to think of it as the graying of Lambert's Cove. It was aging as we were, though from time to time there were portents that our beach was au courant as any in the modern world; sailboats, jet-skis, and boom boxes.

One summer a few years ago was the summer of the pregnant women, wonderful to watch in their colorful suits as they picked their way carefully down the stones and into the water, where they would float peaceably like turquoise seals. The pregnant women lent a serious air to Lambert's Cove that summer, and of course the next year there were—well, how many?—*scores* of infants sleeping under beach umbrellas. Many of them were topless, and earned more attention than the young women sunning themselves near the Coca-Cola river.

And last year? Like Hemingway's war, the beach was there but we didn't go to it any more, except late in the afternoon, round about dusk. Too many crowds, too much noise, boats in the cove. The beach has become a casualty.

Topless windsurfing: a Vineyard specialty.

Ward Just has lived in Lambert's Cove for ten years. He is the author of eight novels and three collections of short stories of which the latest, '21', was recently published by Houghton Mifflin Co.

A Menemsha tapestry.

On Solitude

BY BARBARA LAZEAR ASCHER

When I tell my friend who is walking toward her guest house arms full of Pratesi sheets, that I don't allow summer house guests, she stops and addresses me with a mixture of incredulity and disapproval. "But what do you say when a cousin calls from California and asks to come East to spend a few days?" I shrug. She grows more agitated. "What about your best friend who happens to be city-bound in August? Not even a weekend? You wouldn't even offer her an overnight?"

"Nope."

I am more direct now than I was when I first decided to change our summer lifestyle. Then, my responses were as weighted with guilt as Goethe's letters to abandoned friends back in the court of Weimar—those not invited along when under an assumed name he caught a night mail coach bound for Italy and solitude.

"I am so happy that you have taken my disappearance as well as I hoped you would," he wrote, probably knowing full well that they considered his actions selfish and bohemian. "Please make my peace with any heart that may have been offended at it. I did not mean to upset anyone and I cannot yet say anything to justify myself. God forbid that the motives which led to my decision should ever hurt the feelings of a friend."

God forbid. How to justify to friends a desire to spend August solely in the company of family? It takes time for words to rendezvous with resonance of the heart. Time and age for action to catch up with instinct. This seems especially true when to answer the call of instinct would take us from the table of convention. When we are told that the call is for us, it's hard to ask gracefully, "May I be excused?"

The decision to boycott houseguests was not a sudden one. It followed a slow, unplanned ebb into solitude. It was a preference that grew as I left my frenzied twenties and thirties, a time of acquiring friends and approval. It was not that we didn't enjoy the camaraderie of summer cocktail parties, the chance to catch up with friends whose busy city lives had kept us apart, to engage in that particular kind of vacation conversation that moves easily from thought provoking philosophizing to idle gossip. It was not a conscious decision to participate less. We simply allowed the sea to take hold.

At six PM summer sky turns Vineyard Sound to gold and then to hues of rose and purple. Other skippers furl sail, head home, don red trousers and hoist gin and tonics. We were alone out here, left to ourselves and each other. Without plans, subterfuge, or stealth we had sailed into the bliss of solitude. We may not have known it yet, but we were developing a taste for solitary confinement—the kind that frees the soul.

However, seclusion excludes. Your retreating back will be pelleted by buck shots of accusations. "You seem to have dropped out of our lives." The hurt voice on the other end of the phone belongs to the doyenne of our summer community's social life. She informs me that it is unseemly to flaunt a persistent preference for privacy, for the company of one's spouse and child above all others. I stare at my feet, the toes begin to turn inward. I have automatically assumed the posture of a two-year-old who has been caught being herself. In my forties, more and more I am caught being myself.

I would make amends. I would fashion the moral equivalent of Goethe's letters. I'd give a cocktail party. I invite my caller immediately. She accepts with pleasure and adds, "You know I love you, darling, otherwise I wouldn't tell you these things."

I list my guests on paper and my sins in my mind. Who did I think I was, giving myself over to Henry James and Jane Austen and Chekhov, and lovemaking and long naps after lunch? What had I done to deserve silence and daydreams? I would confess self-indulgence and redeem the sated self. I ordered Scotch. (On the Vineyard real men still drink Scotch. If they've ever heard of a spritzer, they probably think it's something their wives use in the garden or on their hair.) I dreaded the event. When it occurred, I had a good time. We like our friends.

And yet, was the pleasure of their company a match for the enchantment of an unscheduled evening, following an unplanned day? If the breezes blew from the right direction, we might sail to Cutty-hunk, the neighboring island of my childhood and return with baskets full of the bounty of the sea and my parents' garden. Once home, there is no need to take off the favorite old salt encrusted sweater. Pots are set to boil, a bit of water for the fresh corn, wine for the mussels. One hand stirs while the other holds a book and Jane Austen's garden paths take on the perfumes of barnacle and brine.

When it is time for attention to turn exclusively to family, there's no need to show Mr. Darcy to the door, I just close the book and we're alone. If there are the two or three of us at dinner, conversation is a matter of choice, not form. If the spirit moves us, we can just stare out silently at the fog as it tucks us in for the night. We toast each other in all the languages we can muster (two and a half). And reach across the table for a hand, a

Observing the awesome pounding of the surf is often best enjoyed in solitude.

Stillness at Quitsa.

ritual. A way of saying, I love you. Thank you for this moment. It would not happen with guests present because the most important work of a hostess is to make the invited feel included, and the deep familial secrets of love are by nature exclusive.

As darkness falls, we light a fire to catch and dry the evening dampness persistently pushing its way beneath our doorstep. We listen for the whippoorwill. If we're lucky that's our only call. We step out on the deck to bid reluctant farewells to day and light. Fog falls on our eyelashes and settles there. We listen for the Menemsha bell buoy that has sung us to sleep for all the years of our lives together. Far across the water, where bay meets open sea, comes the haunting sound of the Texas Tower foghorn that filled us with loneliness as we lay in the separate beds of our childhoods. These are the sounds and memories that bind families and give them a sense of place. Would they be heard above the happy chatter shared with visiting friends?

We have determined that August is the time for life to have its way with us. Given our druthers, each day would be lived in response to wind and tide rather than schedule and engagement. This cannot be done when there are ferries to be met and meals to be planned. You can't live off the whims of blueberry bushes, wild sorrel, and whatever happens to be in the lobster pot when there are expectant mouths about the table. You can't bask in silence when ears await the news of your life. Our friends deserve better than the passivity we pursue. They deserve our attention—and they've got it. But not for these thirty-one days. Perhaps before departing for this summer's retreat, I'll leave a recording of that plaintive "golden oldie" on my answering machine: "See you in September, or lose you to a summer love . . ."

And lose them I might, to all those kind people with generous hearts and guest houses. But what I have gained is the peace that comes from moving on the wind's way and sharing days with birds, berries that ripen in the sun, deer that walk in the forests, and a husband and daughter whose lives are as overextended, over-scheduled, and remote as all Manhattan lives the remaining eleven months of the year. These thirty-one days are for silences and the rhythms of sea and heart. Rhythms that can't be heard above the spatter of eggs being fried for hungry house guests.

Barbara Lazear Ascher, frequent contributor to The New York Times *and author of two books of essays,* Playing After Dark *and* The Habit of Loving, *has been coming to Menemsha every summer since 1967—a mere 23 Vineyard years compared to her husband's 66.*

From *The Habit of Loving,* Copyright © 1989 by Barbara Lazear Ascher.

Chilmark schoolkids enjoy a winter recess between classes.

Vineyard Seasons

BY SUSAN BRANCH

Up until eight years ago, when I moved myself lock, stock & barrel from California to Martha's Vineyard, I had never actually *seen* a change of season. I had lived a one-season kind of life, pretty much a constant summer, on the California coast. We had only slightly varying degrees of hot: very, very hot, plain hot, or hot-lite. Instead of seasons, unless you counted "fire season," we had certain "conditions": Santa Ana Winds, which made it windy-hot, and when put together with "fire season," made for "dangerous conditions." We had air quality (smog) alerts which meant: don't drive, don't exercise, keep your children indoors, and above all, try not to breathe. There was "earthquake weather," the weirdest weather of all, not a sound, no peeping birds, no wind, just dead eerie silence, and my cats running up and down the tree like they had been put on fast-forward . . . with a very strange look in their eyes, stranger even than usual. Once in awhile, if we all prayed together, it would rain. That's about it. There were other oddities, Tule (pron. Too-ly) Fog, for example, a low, crawling wall of fog from the San Joaquin Valley that caused 35-car pileups. But, for the most part there were simply days and days of perfect sunshine, on and on, forever and ever. The weatherman was lonely and ignored because who cared? There was no "Ghiorse Factor" —there was no factor at all. We all knew what the weather was going to do. Nothing. It *would* be warm.

There was no rush of "Spring Bloom," there were no winter nights where the stars glitter hard in the black sky, no one was particularly *excited* when summer weather came and worst of all, the leaves never changed color. And maybe those things don't seem important, maybe they even bore you if you've always had them, but to me it's like the difference between a song with one note, and the other kind. On Martha's Vineyard, if all else fails, at least the seasons change. And you arc forced to sit up and take note and change the way you eat, dress, drive, live and arrange your house if you want to, basically, survive.

Things just didn't seem *right* to me in California. It *bothered* me when I planted daffodils on November 1st and they'd be up and going by the 15th. I really *wanted* that "First Blush of Spring," I wanted the surprise and the celebration, I wanted *order*, a time to every purpose under heaven, all things in their right and God-ordered time and I wanted the daffodils to come up in *April*. I suppose I could have *planted* them in April, but instead, when the time was right, I packed up and brought myself to the place where I felt sure I would find the things that seemed to be missing.

Rosa Rugosa swayed by a Northeast breeze in mid-May at Harthaven.

Beach Plum blossoms overlooking Stonewall beach.

Springtime at Cannonball Park in Edgartown.

I had no idea what I was getting myself into. The changes in the weather meant things I'd never even considered. I studied the weather reports and chose my news station based completely on the weatherman. I didn't know how to dress in winter and had to call people and ask. I had to do this two winters in a row, because by the time the second winter had gotten here, I had forgotten what I did the first time around. I'd never heard of storm windows, mud porches, leaf raking, Rusty Jones, humidifiers, dehumidifiers, or oil heat. The cost of oil had never meant a thing to me. There were no basements or attics in California, and your yard furniture stayed in your yard year- round. I had never tasted an oyster, clam or mussel; I'd never even *seen* a whole live lobster with claws and head and all (or a dead one either). I had never fed wild birds, never seen a Cardinal, or a flock of geese, or a swan in its natural habitat. (I did see a swan on the pond of the Beverly Hills Hotel once, but its wings were clipped, otherwise I'm sure it would have flown the coop, so to speak.) *Worst* of all, I'd never seen a firefly, which I LOVE, and feel sorry for myself and all others who had to grow up without them. (I think fireflies might be a very good reason to have children, to share the magic of those twinkling lights.) I had never worn *through* several pairs of leather slippers and I'd definitely never, ever worn *out* a leather jacket. In California, Christmas often meant a swim in the pool after opening presents. It definitely did *not* mean sauntering on a tiny Main Street, humming Christmas Carols while little flakes of snow floated down and landed in a sparkle on shoulders and hair, and it certainly never meant running to the window to watch the horse-drawn wagon from Nip-N-Tuck Farm jingle bell down the street, full of happy, bundled, singing people. There had never been a special *reason* to heat up the kitchen (God forbid, actually!) by making soup and baking muffins. Christmas lights in California seem almost stagnant in the warm night air compared with the magical twinkling that takes place on Main Street in Vineyard Haven. I never before experienced that newfound feeling of freedom that comes once a year when winter finally ends and we break loose into the outdoors again.

Holidays are very different here; it seems like people jump to the idea of a celebration. Memorial Day, for example —not only do we remember the past and visit the graves, but flags fly, we march in parades, summer begins, stores open, picnics are mandatory, a little sailing is in order, and everybody has to eat asparagus.

The vegetable section at Cronigs is a very good season "marker," from fresh Island blueberries and corn on the cob, to those little pink golf balls labeled "tomatoes" in winter; I learned to eat seasonally. Those golf balls of winter just make the juicy tomatoes of summer that much more delicious. We wait with excitement and daily visits to the garden for the first tomato to ripen. I call Joe down at the Black Dog to tell him of the "harvest," so he'll get home early. We savor it, chopped with a little olive oil and black pepper, a splash of good red wine and a bit of salt. Yum! I don't think I actually ever *savored* a tomato in California. In fact, my sister Mary called last summer and said, "What's so good about the tomatoes out there? Are they some special kind, or what? I don't think we get the same kind you do." Apparently I'd written so much in my cookbooks about these wonderful summer tomatoes that she imagined we had something they don't! One must eat pink golf balls in winter to truly enjoy a real tomato. And that's what it's really all about, the change. We're not stuck with one note—we have the full song with the high notes and low notes and a lovely intricate melody in between. We have texture.

From this vantage point, I'd say it was Fall I would have missed the most, if I had known what I was missing. It's my favorite time of year. It's the season that makes the constant cleaning of the humidifiers worth it, the one that is the light at the end of a summer filled with crowds, traffic, lines, and other similar irritations. (Summer is my least favorite season, I think I've had enough of it!) To me, Autumn is poignant, it's delicate, the beginning of the end (which of course, is the beginning of the beginning). The first time I feel "fall in the air" my energy level doubles. I scramble to the Farmer's Market to get the last of the zinnias and sunflowers and those final last tomatoes to freeze for winter sauces. The Farmer's Market is so quiet, so remarkably uncrowded that I stay to talk to all the people I had to throw money at and grab the goods from during the summer! When the Farmer's Market is but a seasonal memory, I love to go to Morning Glory Farm and see the great display of pumpkins and Mums, pick up that still-warm pumpkin bread and the last of the basil. I rev up my Cuisinart to make my pesto for Christmas; my blueberry patch is already stripped bare, the fruit is frozen for surprise winter pies. I love to air-dry my quilts on the chilly days to make them fresh for the bed, get the wood pile in order, drive North Road to Menemsha to watch the sun set red and eat a lobster on the beach. I adore going for long walks in the woods, the little winds make the hairs on my arms stand on end; I spread my arms and I can almost fly. Sometimes I surprise the geese at Tashmoo Farm, and they take off, flapping wildly in honking unison, or I see them come in for a landing on the Pond. I'm in just the right place at just the right time.

This fall I moved into town, to the historic district of Vineyard Haven. This neighborhood has something my other one didn't, HUGE flocks of birds, I mean *large* gangs of them, that swoop and dive

The Farmer's Market in West Tisbury; choices galore.

A carrot top, mums and pumpkins accent an autumnal fiesta at Morning Glory Farm in Edgartown.

81

Ivy-covered walls at Seven Gates Farm in October.

as a group. The ultimate air show. They hang out together in a giant tree a little down the street and are so noisy I don't know how the people there can sleep. I hear them from inside the house. But I'm like a child when I see them, pointing with excitement and saying as in *Dick and Jane*, "Look, Look!" This fall I was rolling around on my new lawn (new to me), playing with my cat, looking up into the 150 year old trees, watching the leaves come down. It was sunny, a tiny chill in the air, but warm so close to the ground. And all of a sudden the church bells started ringing; over the treetops the spire of the Tisbury town hall was perfect and white against the blue sky and my senses were alive with the beauty of it all. It was what I always dreamed it would be like. It was very romantic, and to top it off, I was on an Island. I used to see calendars, in gas stations in California, that had pictures of Fall scenes, showing little

villages surrounded with these wildly colored trees. I came to the conclusion that they were fake; that the pictures were taken with a special lens or that it had colored paper over it or something, but, definitely, they were fake. I just couldn't *believe* that those colors could be real.

Fall is like a long glorious march toward the biggest fiesta of them all, Christmas! Certain scenes stand out—the gnarled old tree in Edgartown where they've hung loads of wax or wooden pears and standing on one of the twisted branches is a brightly painted "partridge" —lit by one spotlight, it's just elegant and completely dependent on that old and stately fruit tree. The Christmas Parade in Edgartown stands out mostly because of the faces of the children, little red cheeks and noses sticking out of funny knitted caps, the look of awe mixed with a kind of hysteria on the faces of the

Ripple wind, still water.

Fred Fisher takes the reins for a Christmas sleigh ride at Nip-N-Tuck farm.

Christmas Eve along Main Street in Vineyard Haven; all is calm, all is bright.

A freak November snowfall on Franklin Street in Tisbury.

8-year-olds as Santa comes riding down the street. The clean, simple lines of the Congregational Church in West Tisbury, sitting tidily in the snow; the silly, quiet, gaiety going on across the street in the yard of the Field Gallery. Martha's Vineyard is pure unadulterated magic at times, most times, and I feel blessed to be a part of it.

Lots of "old timers" (I think that means anyone here over 10 years) cry out at the changes, they remember the good old days as the only good ones. The way I see it is that we still have days and days of perfect peace and many, many moments where we can still feel very close to nature. What more can anyone ask for? It's a crowded world wherever you go. Yes, protection for this place is the most important thing, take it from someone who grew up in the "country"—the idyllic countryside known as the San Fernando

Valley—where we moved in 1953 so we could have wide open spaces and so my dad could see his mountain vistas. Now, those mountains, which are a 15 minute car ride away, are invisible, blocked by smog. One wide street was like a tunnel, the old oaks had grown so large they had bent over the street to touch each other. What a beautiful street that was. One day I drove out there and they were GONE—I guess they were in the way of some development so somebody brilliant just got rid of them, leaving no trace of the 3 mile shady road I loved. And nobody even *asked* me!

It can happen, and it *does* happen, and it *will* happen if we don't pay attention, if we don't stand up and say NO, read my lips, N.O. (That's N period O period.) So, that's all I have to say about that. But as for today, it is 31 degrees and the sky is blue, but for some reason that I still don't

84

An omnipresent Santa appears Islandwide during December. Here he leads the annual Edgartown parade during the "Christmas in Edgartown" weekend at mid-month.

quite understand (upper altitude wind currents?), it is snowing. It is winter, Martha's Vineyard belongs just to us. I think I'll go for a walk.

Oops! One more thing before I go. I just want to say that there are things I truly miss about California, mostly my big wonderful family and my dearest oldest friends who are still there in that constant sunshine and loving it. A place, its seasons, the celebrations are one thing, but old friends and family are quite another. Both can tug at your heart, and do mine. I just wanted to say that. Bye. ♡

Susan Branch, author of two handwritten and beautifully watercolored cookbooks, Heart of the Home *and* Vincyard Seasons *(Little, Brown) has recently completed her third,* Christmas: from the Heart of the Home, *also published by Little, Brown.*

The Black Dog Restaurant on a slow day in January.

Chilmark pastorale.

A Tall Island, Indeed

BY HARVEY WASSERMAN

One fine summer day the sands and surf of Lucy Vincent beckoned.

So I stole away from our rented Menemsha house and talked my way past the guard at the town parking lot. We hadn't had time to get our access permit yet, but I did have our house lease, which the guard accepted with the admonition that I get to town hall tomorrow.

Free at last, I began walking up the path toward this magnificent Chilmark beach, a stretch of sand and surf that lives deep in my soul.

With the sun pounding down and the surf breaking ever louder, I planned to walk those timeless free miles, right to the cliffs and rocks of Windy Gates, or left toward Katama and the Great Tisbury Pond, where the cut could be a raging torrent, or a mere trickle, or even a solid sandy bridge, and I could decide there whether to amble on further or turn around and come back or just lie down and sleep for a while.

But as the sandy path fed into the Vincent Beach a woman with an inappropriate scowl came marching out. Her hands were cupped and full of sand, on top of which I saw something most unwelcome—a hypodermic needle. I hadn't read of any medical waste washing up here, but certainly knew it was happening in New York and New Jersey. It is, after all, the same ocean.

The sight did not ruin my afternoon. We've come to accept these things as part of life in post-Reagan America. It's been my line of work for some time to fight these kinds of issues politically. We all know by now that our home is a small, thoroughly intertwined planet. There was clearly no choice but to accept this sort of thing happening on the Vineyard as a matter of course. But certainly it hurt.

So did the sign to my right, announcing the long walk to Windy Gates was now off limits, a private beach. I stood motionless and looked at it for quite a while. I've been coming here since 1972 and there are big magic boulders and mud pools and that beautiful rocky stretch down towards the end that are intimate cosmic companions. I don't know how I could leave the Vineyard without visiting them.

But I obediently went to the left, past the beautiful little hillock we call South Mountain. On New Year's Eve, 1980, I spent a frigid metaphysical night there, meditating and waiting for sunrise, which came more powerfully than I could ever have dreamed. Now that mound is off-limits too, crumbled by so many pilgrims like myself it's in danger of disappearing altogether.

I didn't have much time anyway, so I limited my pilgrimage to a short eastward trek.

But later in the week, when our sticker was in order, I came back with my twin girls, anticipating that long free stride toward Katama. Ambling along with my daughter Abbie on my shoulders, we passed South Mountain. I was overjoyed at being able to share this with her. My plan was to walk as far toward Katama as the spirit beckoned, then to return for Annie and walk her down there as well.

My girls were now just over two years old. This was their first time at the beach, any beach, and was perfect for me that they were starting here.

We payed our respects to South Mountain, then to the volleyball game just beyond.

In the distance stretched those precious

A stretch of sand and surf that lives deep within the soul.

miles of open beach. But as we walked a guard rose from his chair and asked me where I was headed. I was stunned.

My first encounter with a guard on a beach was like a scene from Camus. I was walking very much alone at Gay Head when a gentleman arose from his chair to inform me that the stretch of pure white sand and surf from whence I'd come was fine, but that beyond a certain imaginary line I could not go.

I laughed then. It seemed so utterly incongruous for this fellow to sit on folding metal in the middle of that white expanse and divide one empty stretch of beach from another, that I really didn't care.

But today I had Abbie on my shoulders and I was too stunned to say anything. It was inconceivable to me that we would have to turn back, and I became suddenly disoriented.

Fortunately, at that precise moment, two buddies came along and named someone down the beach we are all going to see, befuddling the guard, allowing us to pass.

And a fine afternoon we had. Abbie fell asleep on my shoulders and the cut was all sanded over. When we arrived, she waded in the warm, rusty waters of that gorgeous pond. Then we walked back, having seen those for whom we came.

By the time we arrived at South Mountain it was that moment of the late afternoon when a chill makes itself felt. On cue the entire gathering of sunbathers arose as a single organism, gathered its blankets and baskets, and headed out. That used to be my signal to settle in and wait for sunset.

But now I had kids. So I promised Annie we'll make the same trek another day, and we proceeded home.

The question of these beaches no

A beach guard at Lucy Vincent; one should never be where one does not belong.

A "perfect 10" beach day in Chilmark.

Island activism.

Anti-war sentiment is draped over the Gazebo at Ocean Park during a 1982 peace rally.

petroleum giants? If the Valdez had run aground off Provincetown, the slick would have stretched all the way to the Carolinas. Every beach here, private or otherwise, would have been drenched in goo.

And what will we be breathing along these beaches? We love the Vineyard in part for its delicious isolation. But we now must grudgingly admit that like everything else in our modern ecology, that separateness is an illusion.

In fact, the Vineyard is periodically downwind from any number of ill-conceived and badly built nuclear power plants. To the north, in the line of fire from winter nor'westers, is Pilgrim, an accident waiting to happen. Due west are three Connecticut reactors at Millstone and yet another at Haddam Neck. Flying once in a small private plane we passed directly over the three aptly named Mill-stone containment domes. I held my breath. It was a futile but involuntary response.

To the south and a bit west is Shore-ham, over which decades of bitter battle have been fought. The citizens of Long Island have shouted for years that their homes cannot be evacuated in the face of a meltdown.

The fight—which probably won't be definitively resolved until well into the next century—has direct bearing on the survival of all Vineyarders. Depending on wind direction, a meltdown at Shore-ham could easily do more damage here than on much of Long Island. The same could be true of Indian Point, sixteen miles north of Manhattan, whose lethal fallout could easily reach the Vineyard within a day given the "right" wind patterns. Large quantities of fallout are still being detected hundreds of miles from Chernobyl, and there is no reason why American down winders—Vineyarders or otherwise—should be immune.

Indeed, in 1979, while writing a book in Chilmark, the meltdown at Three Mile Island made me think very directly of what it might be like to try to leave this enchanted place in the face of a fallout cloud. In a two-day period the fallout from TMI flew virtually all directions on

longer being open and free lingers. But it's the hypodermic needle that really matters. I can always come back in September and walk the Vineyard's magnificent shoreline to my heart's content. The question of private beaches, something I always considered a contradiction in terms, can wait for the time being.

The real question is: What will I encounter on them? More medical waste? Piles of bottles and cans, the more mundane flotsam and jetsam of a throw-away culture? Some raw sewage from the over-burdened treatment facilities of the Cape or Long Island? Or how about a massive oil slick from Exxon or one of its sibling the compass. It never really reached the Vineyard with any force, but it was detected passing through the Berkshire foothills in western Massachusetts. Heightened infant death rates showed up in southern Canada, easily within a TMI-centered radius that would include the Vineyard.

Other air-borne plagues can reach here too. Acid rain has now spread throughout the world, emanating not only from Ohio but from huge coal-burners in the southwest, which threaten the Grand Canyon, and in Florida, where damage is being done to the Everglades. Back yard lawns everywhere are turning to moss and copper pipes are leeching blue water into the sink due to overly acidic water in the ground.

What exactly comes to the Vineyard is anyone's nightmare. But come it does.

And fight back we must. That the summers here have become so crowded as to prompt a proliferation of private beaches is one thing, an issue for communal debate.

But the plagues of a global ecology being plunged into decline reside in another dimension. No hand-painted "keep off" sign or lonesome guard seated on a stretch of beach can protect this place, however special, from what our species is doing to this planet as a whole.

The Vineyard resides deep in our hearts not because it is different from the rest of the planet, but because so many of the Earth's special treasures are crammed into the precious corners of this place. Of course it needs to be preserved, like the rare jewel it is, with acts of Congress and acts of sanity. (Why, in God's name, are they still bombing Noman's? How do they continue to get away with it?!?).

But even more so, each wound to the ecology of this enchanted place should remind us a hundredfold that on a planet overbrimming with inappropriate technologies and greed, there are no more islands. Every day one of Martha's sweet scrub oaks dies from midwestern sulfur emissions. A Tisbury squirrel is killed by a random isotope from Pilgrim or Millstone. A Chappy bluefish succumbs to solid waste from New Bedford (or Chappy itself). A Vineyard native has his or her

life shortened by ozone from an automobile in Manhattan or New Haven, Oak Bluffs or Vineyard Haven.

None of this is any longer new, of course. We all know how much we need our sanctuaries, our Vineyards of the soul and spirit.

Can we find a way to both protect and share them?

None of us needs to be preached to about the vile energies that are destroying our garden planet. But so much rare power focuses here, so many spiritual resources, with the reverence so many feel for her, perhaps a reversal, a salvation, an ecological epiphany of sorts can beam out of Martha's heart and into the surrounding biosphere.

Maybe it's too much to ask, really. It's a tall order.

But she's a tall Island.

A historian, journalist and activist, Harvey Wasserman's writings include four books and numerous articles published in periodicals around the world. He speaks extensively on campuses and in the media on American history and global ecology. His first book, Harvey Wasserman's History Of The United States was re-published in 1989 and he has been termed "the leading historian for a new, emerging generation." He lives in, of all places, Columbus, Ohio with his family.

"Earth Day," April 22, 1990, brought together many environmentally concerned participants at the regional high school.

Harvey "Sluggo" Wasserman and the "twinsies."

Vacation Cause & Effect

BY ART BUCHWALD

At last—the vacation is about to begin. The summer homes have been reopened, the tennis courts swept, the fish are jumping and the voice of the turtle can be heard in the land.

Zeigfrass entered the kitchen at 8.

"Shall we jog through the woods and sing with the birds?" I asked him.

"We can't," he replied. "I just stopped by to take you to a meeting to 'Save the Bluefish.'"

"I didn't know they were endangered."

"They're not," he said. "But somebody has to save them anyway. People are pulling them out of the sound as if there were no tomorrow."

"When will the meeting be over?"

"About 10."

"Good, then we'll play some tennis."

"We can't at 10. There's a demonstration in front of the town hall to protest the zoning commission's decision to allow 30 town houses to be built on the waterfront. We expect you to be there."

"Lunch," I said, "I'm free to go to lunch at the Black Dog with my children, aren't I?"

Despite the fact that Art comes to the Vineyard to vacation, he spends much time supporting Island charities, most notably, the Community Services. He is the auctioneer extraordinaire for the annual "Possible Dreams" and helped raise over fifty thousand dollars for a single item in 1988; a private concert of three songs and a peanut butter sandwich, by Carly Simon.

Zeigfrass looked at his list. "No. We're having a strategy meeting with our lawyer to see how we can limit the rate of growth in East Chop. He's going to tell us how to tie the developers up in knots."

"I know I shouldn't ask this, but how am I fixed for the afternoon?"

Zeigfrass said, "At 2 o'clock I've got you down for an anti-apartheid demonstration in front of a South African guy's summer home."

"What a coincidence. That's exactly when I was going to the beach. What happens at 3?"

"We're raising money for a boys' and girls' club at the Old Whaling Church. Then we go over to the sewage disposal plant and block the entrance gate with our bodies."

"Will I be home for dinner?"

"If you don't get arrested you will. You know there is a potluck dinner at the American Legion for the Order of the Sisters of Massachusetts tonight?"

"No one told me," I said. "Hey look, I only have a couple of weeks, and while I am sympathetic to all your causes, you've got me doing just what I do at home, only more so."

"You can go sailing or play golf if you want to," Zeigfrass said, "but that isn't what vacations are all about. If you can't be counted when we're trying to save the environment, then why don't you just go snorkeling and forget about the world you inhabit."

"I'm all for the environment, but if I spend my whole time protecting it, when do I get to enjoy it?"

"I never thought I would hear you say that you would rather ride the waves than save an osprey from extinction."

"I didn't say that," I protested.

"You said something almost like it," Zeigfrass retorted. "Look, if you want to have a good time on your vacation, that's your business, but you're the one who

will have to answer to your grandchildren 40 years from today."

"You're right. Why would I want to have a good time when there is so much work left to do? I'm willing to help out. The ocean will always be there, if not during my time here—then somebody else's."

Zeigfrass handed me a bridge table.

"What am I supposed to do with this?"

"We're going down to Main Street to collect signatures."

"What for?"

"I haven't decided yet."

A nationally syndicated humorist, Art Buchwald spends his summers in Vineyard Haven. Aside from playing tennis with Mike Wallace, he finds the time to preside with his gavel at the annual fundraiser, the "Possible Dreams Auction," in Edgartown. He is the author of many books, the most recent being, Whose Rose Garden is it Anyway? *(G. P. Putnam's Sons).*

Due to his busy schedule of summer causes, Art hardly ever gets the chance to enjoy some fun in the sun.

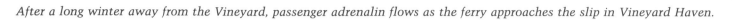

After a long winter away from the Vineyard, passenger adrenalin flows as the ferry approaches the slip in Vineyard Haven.

A Haven on the Vineyard

BY MIKE WALLACE

Something extraordinary happens each time I leave my "real" life in New York City and arrive—at home—in Vineyard Haven. All the magic of my schoolboy excursions to the Vineyard comes flooding back, all the early memories.

I remember, from my first visit to the Island when I was in my teens, the gulls soaring above the ferry on the way over from Woods Hole; I can hear the chains and the gangplanks; I can see the people and bikes getting off; I recall the salty smell of the sea.

For some inexplicable reason, whenever I get here and settle in for a while, the world outside evaporates. The Vineyard is the only place I know where I somehow feel totally, utterly relaxed; people who know me from that other world find the change difficult to fathom in a person they normally perceive as driving and intense.

Liftoff.

When I'm here I feel a peculiar sense of roots. My childhood home was Brookline, so perhaps it's because of my Massachusetts background. But it's also the memory that my mother and father vacationed here each summer, plus the simple fact that the Vineyard represents some of the happiest times of my life. My home today looks out over Vineyard Haven Harbor, and as I watch the ferries come and go each day, all those early feelings still come back.

After spending part of my childhood summers here with my parents in Vineyard Haven, I returned for the first time in 1951 with my first wife and daughter, almost on a whim, and stayed at the Harborside in Edgartown. We spent the next five summers at other spots in Edgar-

Art Buchwald, always entertaining on the court.

Rose Styron, Lucy Hackney, Mike Wallace and Art Buchwald, an inseparable quartet, congregate near the net after a typically hard fought match.

town, but eventually realized that all our best friends lived in Vineyard Haven. I think it's the simplicity here that attracts me. It's such a plain place to live, but plain in the finest sense of the word. Probably because Vineyard Haven is a "dry" town, it has magically retained its essence through the years, it hasn't changed substantially since I first started visiting my folks at the Tashmoo Inn (now the Vineyard Montessori School). There's nothing self-conscious or contrived about Vineyard Haven. It's not advertising itself as "New England." It's kind of an old, comfortable shoe.

Life in the summer, just up Main Street from "downtown Vineyard Haven," often seems like an extended camp reunion. Each morning we pals check with each other to make plans for the day; lunch on the porch at the Vineyard Haven Yacht Club, perhaps the beach for a bit, tennis in the afternoon, then over to Le Grenier or the Blue Water Grille for dinner, where the main question is—who will bring the wine?

But the spine to a Vineyard summer for me is tennis. Almost every day begins with a battle against Bob Brustein up at Beverly Sills' court in Lambert's Cove. He's ten years younger than I, and as I age, and only because of that, I vow, he has become the consistent winner; but whatever the outcome, it's a great way to get the day going.

In the late afternoon, mixed doubles with Art Buchwald, Rose Styron and Lucy Hackney, a different kind of game. Mixed doubles is more sociable; laced with Art's jokes, aimed—successfully—at ungluing our concentration. Occasionally Artie and I take on Rose and Lucy, and chivalry is forgotten. The slices and drop shots for which I am justly famous from Oak Bluffs to Menemsha, come into play, and without apology. To win is all.

Then we go back to Rose's or Lucy's for iced tea and instant analysis of the match just played. If Bill Styron is around, he gets quickly bored and leaves; he doesn't much like instant replays. But he returns when talk turns to politics and gossip. They are all such pals that we're able to rekindle ties each summer as if no time had passed from the previous year, even if we haven't seen each other more than a couple of times during the off-season.

On the Island, while the things I've described take priority, I manage to stay in touch with the "real" world on the other side of Vineyard Sound. Each morning *The Boston Globe* and *The New York Times*, and evenings the TV news fill me in. And it's a joy just to watch the political conventions, or the Ollie North hearings, or the Olympics and not have to actually work them anymore.

I recall on one occasion, though, during the Israeli invasion of Lebanon, CBS convinced me to go because Arafat had declared that I was the only one with whom he would talk. My wife tried to dissuade me; she felt it was too dangerous, and besides it was vacation time and I shouldn't even think of going. I kept saying to myself "I shouldn't do this . . . I shouldn't . . . " because at the end of a "60 Minutes" season I'm fed up with all the travel and cherish the notion of just staying put.

But in the end I convinced myself that this was an opportunity I just couldn't pass up. During a previous "60 Minutes" segment, Arafat had become particularly upset with me about the way the interview had gone, and I had a hard time believing he would grant me another one, but I was curious. So I got myself to Damascus, took a taxi through the night to

Beirut, and when I finally got there, Arafat's press secretary said to me, "What are *you* doing here?" I said "What do you mean, I was told to come!"

And after a couple of days of back-and-forth it became apparent that they wouldn't, in fact, let me see him. So back to the Vineyard with my tail between my legs, to friends who laughed at me for leaving in the first place. Why leave paradise for just another interview?

I've thought occasionally about combining my life here with my profession, but each time I think seriously about it, my instinct tells me to leave the place alone. The only time I was ever really close to doing a "60 Minutes" piece was during the Chappaquiddick episode back in 1969. I moved about the Island talking to various people who were involved, but there was a reluctance to discuss it on camera, and we finally decided to skip it.

Generally, I avoid doing anything about the Vineyard, particularly a "the Vineyard—is—paradise—found" type of puff piece, because that's just not my beat. If another story of considerable proportion came along, like the Kennedy tragedy, I'd probably do it because of my special understanding of the locale, but there really aren't any generic topics here that say to me "you simply must do that story."

In some respects, the Vineyard is a microcosm of the country—with issues like the hospital, drugs, ecology, overdevelopment, economic hardship and affordable housing—but given the choice, I'd prefer doing those stories about other places.

The Vineyard already receives too much media exposure and there's not much we can do about it. It's just too alluring and unique to ignore. It *is* true that many people—too many during the summer—are drawn to visit; the media have created a curiosity, a mystique about the place. People want to find out for themselves what all the commotion is about. Summer residents who vacation here may resent the magazine and television coverage, the hordes of tourists and the traffic jams, but I have trouble believing that the year-rounders really mind, because ultimately it helps their pocket-

books and keeps the Island economically healthy.

The fact that some celebrated people choose to live here creates a sort of curiosity about the place. Why the Vineyard? Possibly because the alternatives aren't as appealing. Nantucket somehow seems a trifle more self-conscious, and the Hamptons are New York City once removed; too trendy and incestuous. And the Cape is just too crowded.

The Vineyard, fortunately, is protected because it's less accessible. At some point, I suppose the Vineyard will reach its people limit and some measures will be taken to prevent further development; already various Island planning boards and commissions have been slowing things down. I just hope they continue turning down Art Buchwald's plea to build a bridge over from Falmouth so he can get more gullible tennis partners who are willing to chase his lobs.

Mike and Mary Wallace, who knew each other for years at work and on the Vineyard, were married at their home in Vineyard Haven in 1986.

Mike Wallace, the well-known, hard-hitting correspondent for 60 Minutes, has covered some of the most important news in modern history, as well as uncovered many of the seamier aspects of our times. His book Close Encounters *(Berkeley Press, 1985) fascinated readers with its behind the scenes accounts of his adventures in televison journalism.*

A staple for all Gingerbread cottages—a comfortable set of rocking chairs.

Oak Bluffs

BY JAMES P. COMER

almost missed the Vineyard. I was busy seeing the country—48 of 50 states—and the world—20 foreign countries. I wanted to see new places. In fact, I had a vacation rule—never go to the same place twice.

But twelve years ago my wife Shirley and I had dinner with our accountant (of all people), and he and his wife raved about the beauty and pleasure of Martha's Vineyard. I had heard about it—travel section of the newspaper or somewhere —and oh, yes, some other friends of ours had a house there. In fact, my wife had proposed visiting the Island previously. But, why? No big deal. She managed to get an agreement to visit out of me while I was not paying much attention to what was being proposed and quickly made reservations before I could tune in and disagree.

We stayed only a week and it rained all but the first and the last day of our visit. But I fell in love with the place. Three yearly month-long rentals later—my travel rule shattered—we decided that if we are going to do this every year we should take up residence. We did—in the Sengekontacket section of Oak Bluffs.

Here we have the best of three worlds— almost equidistant to Edgartown, Vineyard Haven and Oak Bluffs centers. But my heart and soul is in Oak Bluffs, and my car knows.

When I drive to the end of our road, and I am out to mail letters, pick up toiletries, and attend to life's other little things, my car turns left to Edgartown; to pick up *The Boston Globe* on Sunday, it turns right to Vineyard Haven, and Leslie's Drugstore. But for fun and friends, it heads straight to Oak Bluffs center. And

that is what makes Oak Bluffs special. It is the undisputed fun capital of the Island.

The fun is not in the elegant dining available in Oak Bluffs—good food, family style, but not elegant. In fact, there is nothing elegant about Oak Bluffs. There are few stunning vistas. The beach is adequate, but seriously eroding in places. Circuit Avenue, the main street, is . . . uh . . . well, frankly, tacky; thankfully so. (Its claim to fame is the Flying Horses, the oldest carousel in the country. But I like it because it is yesterday's small town main street.) The fun here is in the people and places—active, finger poppin', funny, funky.

My fondest memories of Oak Bluffs are about times with good friends and family, and community fun. Several years ago we spent an evening at David's Island House on Circuit Avenue with our good friends, Bill and Eloise Woods. It was my first week of vacation and I was still carrying the burdens of "the other world." David Crohan, with his seeing eye dog at his side, entertained the audience with his remarkable piano style, finally leading us in a sing-a-long of old favorites, back to the 1940's and 50's, the songs I grew up on. The joy in the room among a large over 40 crowd was almost palpable. I could feel the other world melting away.

The next morning at breakfast my wife and I were describing what a wonderful experience it had been to our then 19 year old son, Brian, and 16 year old daughter, Dawn. They called it "old folks fun" and invited us to join them for "real fun" that evening at the Atlantic Connection, also on Circuit Avenue—if we thought we could keep up. One or two times over the years—well maybe more than that—I

A bird's eye view of downtown Oak Bluffs shows New York Avenue, the harbor and ferry landing.

had pointed up my proficiency as a dancer in my day. They had issued a challenge, and I had to accept.

I danced, and danced, and danced, almost as much as I did in the old days. It was exhilarating—without drugs, illicit or legal, I was high. And oh, the beautiful people in the place. (I admit to being jealous of their beauty and stamina.) Toward the end of the evening Brian looked at me evaluatively, and said of my dancing, "Not bad . . . not bad." That was high praise. Score one for the older generation.

Another of my favorite memories is the evening of the Roberta Flack concert in the Tabernacle at the campground, a circular site that had its beginning as a Methodist revival meeting place in the 1830's. It was a warm August evening, and the crowd gathered early to claim good seats. Families enjoyed picnics here and there on the lawn, surrounded by unique, colorful, and tightly packed gingerbread cottages of summer residents. Ms. Flack was at her best, touching emotional chords in the audience at a depth that probably had not been reached since the revival meetings years before. The families, the site, and the sound together created a warm sense of community that is generally rare in our time, but not rare in Oak Bluffs.

A similar spirit is created on "Illumination Night" at the campground. Every year, after a concert at the Tabernacle, hundreds of people stroll around the area to observe the imaginative lighting designs on the various cottages. The annual fireworks display in Ocean Park has the same effect; with a band concert at the Gazebo, family picnics, children playing, and then, fire works light up the night over Oak Bluffs Harbor and remind us why "the rockets red glare" is a part of our National Anthem.

Almost across the road is a stretch of beach that is the favorite gathering place of African-American residents and vacationers, and for obvious reasons is affectionately referred to by Blacks as the Inkwell. Last summer, 1989, as a health promotion, Dr. Louis Sullivan, Secretary of Health and Human Services, a summer visitor for almost 25 years, led his "Power Walk" in the area. Oak Bluffs was one of the few resort areas that was open to

Crowds gather at Ocean Park to gaze in wonderment at the annual blaze of fireworks, sponsored by the Oak Bluffs' Firemen's Association.

Judge Herbert Tucker with his wife Mary of Oak Bluffs.

Blacks early in this century. It has some fourth generation Black summer residents, as well as a significant group of "Jimmy come latelies"—business, entertainment, professional, and academic people like myself. It has a growing list of prominent permanent residents such as Judge Herbert Tucker, a retired judge on the Island; Dorothy West, perhaps the last of the Harlem Renaissance writers; Vera Shorter, an NAACP leader and the widow of a former superintendent of schools on the Island; Mary Williams, owner of the Carousel Boutique on Circuit Avenue, and others.

It is a unique, interesting, and interested mix—so unique and interested that

they helped to make my book, *Maggie's American Dream*—a story largely about my mother, but symbolic of the African-American struggle—a best seller during a part of the summer of 1989, the only place in the country where this occurred, and perhaps the only place where it could have occurred.

But my favorite spot, and source of pleasurable memories, in all the world is a secret. From Beach Road it is just Sengekontacket Pond. But tucked away in a small alcove not visible from the road it becomes our "Golden Pond." The pond changes faces with the tide, the light, and the weather. A hanging low fog makes me reflective; the lapping waves of high tides are energizing; there is surely a man or woman in the full moon that hangs over "Golden Pond."

The Felix Neck Wildlife Preserve lies across the pond and supplies nature's bounty. A magnificent, beautifully dressed pheasant stopped on our deck rail last summer. Sassy, but alert, it took off when I moved to get my camera. Ducks, geese, and swans parade in caravans back and forth. A mother duck leads her ducklings across the pond in a line so straight

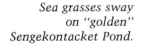

Sea grasses sway on "golden" Sengekontacket Pond.

it would make West Pointers proud. An occasional blue heron, an egret or two, and a host of birds I cannot identify stop by from time to time. The euphony, and sometimes cacophony, of nature sounds make breakfast on the deck very special.

Last summer, Dawn, visiting from Los Angeles, and I maneuvered our small paddle boat around the pond, and then moved in close to observe wild grass growing out of ossified sand. Dawn grew pensive. "What's up?" I asked.

She smiled and said, "Don't ever get rid of this place."

She need not worry. I need it. When things get tough during the year on the mainland, I turn on the picture of "Golden Pond" in my head. That holds

me until I can get back to the fun of Martha's Vineyard, Oak Bluffs, and Sengekontacket Pond.

Dr. James P. Comer is the Director of school development and child study program and Associate Dean of the Yale School of Medicine. His 1988 novel, Maggie's American Dream, *was critically acclaimed. Dr. Comer has also written* Beyond Black And White, Black Child Care, *and* School Power. *He lectures frequently about childhood education, particularly as it applies to the underprivileged.*

Illumination Night in Oak Bluffs, a yearly spectacle that delights one and all.

*Tivoli Day, a mid-September celebration, turns Circuit Avenue in Oak Bluffs
into a teaming mass of humanity.*

Alone and Together

BY JAMES S. GORDON

Twenty-five years ago, on a summer morning, I left Cambridge and medical school to hitchhike to Martha's Vineyard. On the ferry and over. Thumbing up-Island, shaking the city off, alone, and sharply defined in the cooling air. I arrived at a friend's house, welcomed as if I had called, or he had.

I had the same sense last summer. The gravity of the Island larger than its size, pulled at me. A welcome waited. Yet, there was an aloneness. The aloneness was there in the morning as I stretched on my deck and in moments on the beach when the sun shimmered on the water and my mind went into neutral. And it was present at cocktail parties, surprising me as I listened to the stories of tennis and books, houses and children. It was, like the early morning air, sharper and clearer than elsewhere and, though it carried an edge, less painful, more luminous. Once, I watched myself reflected in the

Slowdown, sundown.

pupil of a man I had known from childhood. I turned from him and smiled to see three generations nodding to one another over hors d'oeuvres.

On the Vineyard, this dual sense of aloneness and community, perhaps al-

ways present, works on me like a Zen koan. Friends from Washington who are wrapped in jobs and hidden in their houses in winter, are larger, lighter, more available to each other, and to me, on the beach in summer. It is like camp or college again, a place where people pass one another often and are not afraid of invasion or wary of being drawn off course. The very ease reminds me, at odd moments, of the difficulty that fall will bring. What is so much more important? Or, better still, what can we do to change it?

It is different for people who live on the Island all year, but more, rather than less, acute. Out of season, my friends on the Vineyard oscillate, as if driven by internal storms, between community and aloneness. For three months one woman I know barely sees her best friend and then for a week they are inseparable. Some people gather nightly at the Twelve Step meetings—AA, NA, Adult Children of Alcoholics, Sex and Love Addicts Anonymous—which have, for many, taken the place of church as well as tavern. But during the day and after the meetings they barely speak.

People who fled the mainland twenty years before, to make a new life or new music in a braver more natural world, grow toward one another with time and troubles. Women who still have children and no longer have husbands extend unself-conscious care as well as courtesy in ways that I rarely see on the mainland. I watch as food is prepared, children boarded, and baths are given.

These same women, and their friends, may also shut off their phones. Once, walking in Vineyard Haven I noticed that a longtime resident passed many people in silence. When I asked, he told me that everything is precious on an Island, and fragile most of all, the privacy which had drawn him years ago to the Vineyard. Natives understood. The rules were laid down, in respectful silence, in his first winters. A few casual words to someone with whom he didn't wish to speak might flood the shore of his solitude.

And yet people, silent so often and long, do love to talk. At a party last summer, an Island born man was describing his large, diverse and scandal-prone family. We had just finished comparing notes about a particular criminal type—he was related to one and I knew others—when he paused, surprised at the intimacy, to wonder whether he should be saying these things. I told him that I was interested in stories, not gossip. He paused, we laughed, and once again words flowed between us.

James S. Gordon is a psychiatrist and holistic physician. He practices in Washington, D.C., and teaches at the Georgetown University School of Medicine. Author of The Golden Guru: The Strange Journey of Bhagwan Shree Rajneesh, *he has also written about psychiatry and holistic medicine, homeless and troubled youth, and stress management.*

Best friends.

The pause that refreshes.

No Exit From Eden

BY STAN HART

The Vineyard was always my safety zone or fall-back spot— a place I could retreat to with assurance that everything was really okay. I don't know exactly when the Island took on such a guardian role, but I would suspect it was during my thirteenth year when we moved from New Britain, Connecticut, to southern Maryland. I believe it was at that time when I began to feel that Maryland didn't count, that only the Vineyard counted.

I began to feel that as long as the Island existed I had roots, a base, and, in a sense, an identity. This meant, alas, that what I did in Maryland, and later on in Connecticut, New York, California, or Boston was essentially of little consequence, just the filling of an interlude until I could get home to the Vineyard. And so it was with secondary school, college, the U.S. Air Force, and two good jobs. They were ancillary activities that didn't really matter —the main thing was always there on the Vineyard.

Undoubtedly the Vineyard's pervasive hold on me reflects a youth spent summer after summer, free in the sunshine, if you will, somehow nurtured by the Island's myriad blessings in those prewar years. And nurtured as I was by nature, and simplicity, by fresh air, sun and sea, and a summer house, I felt unique in those days and quite tenacious in my knowledge that I always belonged to the Vineyard.

And it *was* unique. It was a unique adventure coming every summer to Martha's Vineyard. I remember the route down from New Britain, Connecticut, and the dock in New Bedford where we would board either the *Nantucket*, the *New Bedford*, or the *Naushon*. There was a smell to the wharf area, a very salty odor, and the water between the steamer and the dock was slime green and very still like green paint before it's stirred. The giant hawsers that tied the steamer to the pilings smelled of oil and grease and I would stand on the deck at the railing, staring at the cool green water waiting for the sudden whoosh of prop wash, which would tear its placid surface with white foam. Soon, then, the hawsers would go slap into the water, cast loose but falling short of the dock. It would be early June, and we would be off, easing out of our berth on our way to the Vineyard, the fresh smell and taste of ocean air easing over and into the ship.

There was nothing routine about this. You did not just drive down to Wood's Hole and hop on an ugly beetle-shaped ferry as you do now. On those old steamers with their mahogany interiors you "booked passage"—quite another thing from buying a ferry ticket. But what made it most memorable was that in those days before the war and right afterward, it seemed that everyone's face on board was familiar and the odds were that you would know at least half of your fellow passengers. It *was* like coming home and you could feel a palpable camaraderie as people nodded to each other in recognition or shook hands warmly, it having been nine months or so since they had last met. People knew who the others were, and that sense of recognition was key to my early remembrances of the Island. For it was not just on the steamers and later the ferry *Islander*, but it was on land as well. For better or worse you had no anonymity here. Your face if not your

Robin Hyde performing the early July ritual of haying the Keith Farm panorama in Chilmark.

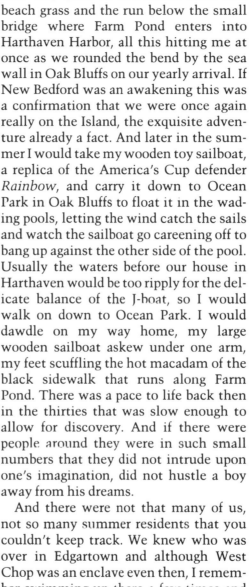

name had been noted over the years, and as the years went by one was bound by a deep sense of belonging.

I remember rather subtle pleasures, too. The odor of sun-baked sand and beach grass and the run below the small bridge where Farm Pond enters into Harthaven Harbor, all this hitting me at once as we rounded the bend by the sea wall in Oak Bluffs on our yearly arrival. If New Bedford was an awakening this was a confirmation that we were once again really on the Island, the exquisite adventure already a fact. And later in the summer I would take my wooden toy sailboat, a replica of the America's Cup defender *Rainbow*, and carry it down to Ocean Park in Oak Bluffs to float it in the wading pools, letting the wind catch the sails and watch the sailboat go careening off to bang up against the other side of the pool. Usually the waters before our house in Harthaven would be too ripply for the delicate balance of the J-boat, so I would walk on down to Ocean Park. I would dawdle on my way home, my large wooden sailboat askew under one arm, my feet scuffling the hot macadam of the black sidewalk that runs along Farm Pond. There was a pace to life back then in the thirties that was slow enough to allow for discovery. And if there were people around they were in such small numbers that they did not intrude upon one's imagination, did not hustle a boy away from his dreams.

June swoon.

And there were not that many of us, not so many summer residents that you couldn't keep track. We knew who was over in Edgartown and although West Chop was an enclave even then, I remember swimming up there a few times and occasionally I'd meet someone from that aloof promontory. In any case, I had seen West Choppers "around." Vineyard Haven and East Chop kids were far more accessible, and I knew most of them. I also knew most of the Chilmark summer people, if only by their faces. Back in the forties and early fifties the summer colony in Gay Head was very small and too remote and there still were only a few

111

Looking down from atop the Gay Head Cliffs.

aries who admired the rare beauty and the peace and quiet of that up-Island area.

And beauty there was. The up-Island South Beach, as an example, was heavy with beach grass and Sahara-like with its dunes and hollows. The upper and lower Chilmark ponds were connected by a navigable stream, which I used to canoe on moonlit nights. Slipping along those still waters right inside the edge of the ocean, I could hear the plangent thud of surf breaking on hard sand to my left and the rustling of herons in the marsh grass on my right. The mosquitoes could be awful but it was like finding a Northwest Passage slipping along those lambent waters. And when I entered upper Chilmark Pond it was always a discovery, consumed with raw nature, each ripple of the pond picking up the moonbeams, and the ocean was white from the light above. I used to think then that I could never leave the Island no matter what. I would never leave to return to school or college or the Air Force or my job. But I always did, assuming that someday I would be back to stay.

We had cousins who owned two camps up on upper Chilmark Pond, and when I

houses along the North Shore. Indeed, when a friend of mine and I walked around the Island in 1947, the North Shore was mostly deserted. And at night sliding up the Sound with the running lights on in our Palmer Scott power boat you seldom saw house lights except at Seven Gates Farm and right around Tashmoo Inlet. The hills of Chilmark were, of course, barren of houses save for one here and there, belonging to some early vision-

Beach Day.

112

was a small boy my parents would take me along to parties at one or the other shacks, as we called them. Before eating we would all row or paddle across to the ocean to swim in the big rolling surf and then, wet and sandy from being tumbled in the foam, we would return to warm ourselves before the fire. Neither shack had inside toilets and the cooking arrangements were very rudimentary, but we always ate very well and if nature called I would hurry down the walk to the outhouse, trying to avoid the prickers in the grass and the mounds of sheep dip that the grazing herd would have scattered all over the land. At night my parents would put me to bed in a loft up over the living room where I would sleep while they reveled below. The loft always smelled of mothballs and canvas and sometimes the fire would emit special oily fumes from the driftwood that someone had collected from the beach. Lying up there pretending to sleep I would hear the grown-ups laughing and singing, singing songs from the Depression such as, "Let's Put Out The Lights and Go To Sleep," one line of which was, "No more parties at the shore, no more staying up till four." I think right then I knew I was in a special world. Others might not be having their parties at the shore, but we were. It seemed that the few of us who had the Vineyard had everything, and that neither a depression nor a war would ever change it.

But prosperity did. Prosperity and people and maybe your friendly banker who was happy to loan you the money for your summer house on beautiful, unspoiled Martha's Vineyard.

I do not know where I can go, should I leave this place. I have married the Vineyard for life and ruefully I admit that if there is any adjusting to be done it must come from me. Already I know that certain things that please my children so much are distasteful to me, my offspring already part of the present leading to the future. I who look to the past, agonizing over the quality of life now departed, cannot become so immobilized as to lose track of those aspects that remain, those aspects still rewarding, still beneficial to

man's well-being. And so I plod along, just a middle-aged man nursing the days of his youth.

I live on, year-round now, having moved here for keeps in 1968. I have a small house in Chilmark on property that I have owned for forty years or so, land that was once my grandfather's. I live in seaside suburbia that for nine months of the year is deserted save for my family and two or three others. But in the summer they are all there, the eager newcomers who have been lured to the Island and who profess to love it as much as I do. Yet

An invitation to Zack's.

113

they don't know what they have missed, and probably happy with their own good fortune, they couldn't care less. And I appreciate them, for surely they are as blameless as they are lucky, just as I was lucky in 1930 when I first came over from New Bedford.

And I still feel lucky. Even though Chilmark has changed from a summer retreat to a summer resort, it has its continuing virtues. There is still the beach, Menemsha Harbor, and for three months or so there is a host of new friends. Although I enjoy privacy I am not a recluse and new friends present a condition I cherish. That said, summer in Chilmark no longer connotes serenity. Today when I think of Chilmark, I do not think of a lone heron picking its way up Doctor's Creek. I am not contemplating oysters, nor do I fancy steamers and a frenzy of blue crabs from Chilmark Great Pond. Alas, Chilmark Great Pond is polluted. Where are the berries and beach plums? I do not hear the underlying thump of the ocean unless I strain to hear it. There is static in the air. People and their machines create a din. The surge of the sea with its wondrous roar of surf was

once so much a part of my consciousness. Today's Chilmark has become a mere country club, and I hear the sound of tennis balls more readily than the caw of the crow. As Chilmark has changed, so have I.

But I can recall it as it was: a waiting woman comes to mind, sunning herself below the cliffs near Windy Gates (which is now off limits), the languid glide of a gull overhead, swallows darting from the sandy heights and later the long walk back through dense overgrowth, and then a quick drive to Mrs. Grieder's diner in Gay Head. Hot dogs never tasted so good. Feeling the salt and sand and the tightness of skin over bodies young and fit, we ate voraciously. And I recall many such times, each one approximating the other in a skein of summers from the late forties through the fifties.

So it is a mixed bag. Trendy behavior and silly customs move in and take over and sometimes we grow wistful. It is not the paradise I had known, held onto while away and suppressed tears over each September when I had to leave. But in the glorious autumn and in late spring there is a bounty that makes it all worthwhile.

Dusty Miller at Quansoo.

And in the winter months when I stroll through town I get that old sense of recognition I used to get in the summer. I feel that I know everyone and everyone knows me and that I am home and what I do here matters very much indeed.

Stan Hart has been a resident of Martha's Vineyard for over sixty years (the last twenty-five year-round). He has worked in the publishing business for ten years, owned a bookstore for ten years and for the last ten years has been writing articles and books. He is the author of Once A Champion, The Martha's Vineyard Affair *and* Rehab *(published in 1988). He is currently Director of Marketing for Edgehill Publications in Newport, Rhode Island.*

Light snow settles gently on Larsen's backyard tableau in Chilmark.

115

Going barefoot is practically mandatory at the entrance to Lambert's Cove Beach.

Going Barefoot

BY JOHN UPDIKE

When I think of the Vineyard, my ankles feel good—bare, airy, lean. Full of bones. I go barefoot there in recollection, and the Island as remembered becomes a medley of pedal sensations: the sandy rough planks of Dutchers Dock; the hot sidewalks of Oak Bluffs, followed by the wall-to-wall carpeting of the liquor store; the pokey feel of an accelerator on a naked sole; the hurtful little pebbles of Menemsha Beach and the also hurtful half-buried rocks of Squibnocket; the prickly weeds, virtual cacti, that grew in a certain lawn near Chilmark Pond; the soft path leading down from this lawn across giving, oozing boards to a bouncy little dock and rowboats that offered another yet friendly texture to the feet; the crystal bite of ocean water; the seethe and suck of a wave tumbling rocks across your toes in its surge back down the sand; sand, the clean wide private sand by Windy Gates and the print-pocked, over-used public sand by the boat dock that one kicked around in while waiting for friends to be deferried; the cold steep clay of Gay Head and the flinty littered surface around those souvenir huts that continued to beguile the most jaded child; the startling dew on the grass when one stepped outside with the first cup of coffee to gauge the day's weather; the warmth of the day still lingering in the dunes underfoot as one walked back, Indian-file, through the dark from a beach party and its diminishing bonfire. Going to the post office in bare feet had an infra-legal, anti-totalitarian, comical, gentle feel to it, in the days before the postal service moved to the other side of Beetlebung Corner and established itself in a lake of razor-sharp spalls. (When Bill Seward ran the postal annex in his store, it was one of the few spots in the United States that delivered mail on Sundays.) Shopping at Seward's, one would not so carefreely have shelled out "Island prices" for such luxuries as macadamia nuts and candied snails had one been wearing shoes; their absence, like the cashless ease of a charge account, gave a pleasant illusion of unaccountability. A friend of mine, who took the photographs in this book, used to play golf at Mink Meadows barefoot. My children and I set up a miniature golf course on a turn-around covered with crushed clam shells; after treading this surface for a while, it did not seem too great a transition, even for a middle-aged father of four, to climb a tree barefoot or go walking on a roof. The shingles felt pleasantly peppery, sun-baked.

These are summer memories, mostly August memories; for that's the kind of resident I was. Now it has been some summers since I was even that, and a danger exists of confusing the Vineyard with my children's childhood, which time has swallowed, or with Paradise, from which we have been debarred by well-known angels. Let's not forget the rainy days, the dull days, the cranky-making crowding, and the moldy smell summer furniture gives off when breezes don't blow through the screen door one keeps meaning to fix. Beach pebbles notoriously dry to a disappointing gray on the mantel. The cozy roads and repeated recreations can begin to wear a rut. One wet summer we all, kids and cousins and friends of cousins, kept walking down through poison ivy, *not* barefoot, to look at a heap of

An optical collusion.

large stones that was either a ninth-century Viking cromlech or a nineteenth-century doghouse, nobody was certain which. Still, there was under it all, fair days and foul, a kicky whiff of freedom, a hint, whispered from the phalanges to the metatarsals, from the calcaneus to the astragalus, that one was free from the mainland's paved oppressions.

Going barefoot is increasingly illegal, and does have its dangers. One house we rented overlooked the Menemsha Bight from a long porch whose spaced boards had the aligned nicety of harp strings or the lines of type in a book. One of my boys, performing some stunt on these boards, rammed splinters into the soles of his feet so deeply a doctor across the Island had to cut them out with a surgeon's knife. I wonder if even the most hardened hippies still pad along the tarry streets of Oak Bluffs barefoot as they used to. At Jungle Beach, I remember, nudity spread upward to the top of the head and became doctrinaire. But then nudism, interwoven with socialism in the Island's history, has always had a doctrinaire side. Being naked approaches being revolutionary; going barefoot is mere populism. "Barefoot boy with cheek of tan" was a rote phrase of my own childhood, quaint even then. But that boy existed and can be seen, not

The Kelly House on a rainy day; all dressed up but nowhere to hide.

Summer fun at its best, without clothes and/or shoes.

only in illustrations of Mark Twain but also in Winslow Homer's level-eyed etchings and oils of his contemporary America, a place of sandy lanes and soft meadows. There are few places left, even summer places, where one can go barefoot. Too many laws, too much broken glass. On Long Island, the cuffs of one's leisure suit will drag on the ground, and on the Cape, pine needles stick to the feet. Even on Nantucket, those cobblestones are not inviting. But the presiding spirits of Martha's Vineyard, willfully and not without considerable overhead, do preserve this lowly element of our Edenic heritage: treading the earth.

John Updike used to summer in Chilmark, but now lives year-round on the North Shore of Massachusetts. He is the father of four children and the author of over thirty books, and is one of the most respected authors of our time.

Muscovi ducks dare to go barefoot near the Coast Guard station in Menemsha.

An important discussion at the Menemsha Market.

A Journey Home

BY JOHN HOUGH, JR.

It is about 500 coastal miles from Washington to the Vineyard, a mental leap I'd become accustomed to making. Daydreaming on a summer morning, I rode the back of an imaginary south wind, racing above the sweep of the coastline till it curled east and then south, doubling back into the emerald-blue waters of Vineyard Sound. I was there in a wink. The wind set me gently down, say, on the knoll by my great-grandfather's house in North Tisbury.

It sometimes seemed almost incredible to me that there could *be* a Vineyard. Once when I was in New York City, walking as night fell on a crowded street in Greenwich Village, threading through the slow-moving clumps of people, the ripe sour smells of scraps from the vegetable stalls, the noise, a thought startled me: at this moment the spring peepers, the pinkletinks, are singing. They are filling the still night air with their silver, sleigh-bell cries, rippling up from the pond, from the ravine, magic afloat in the woods. It hardly seemed possible.

I thought of the house where I'd lived, standing gaunt and straight on its hump rising out of the woods, heaving its sharp roof against the hard sky. A sassafras grove huddles in front; the late sunlight gilds their trunks, and in October their leaves are salmon-pink mittens. From the ridge above, where the dirt road undulates down like a ribbon, you can see the old Norton place, square and snug with its red roof, and Vineyard Sound beyond, a blue fairway where sails glide, slivers of pearl. There's more, of course. The golden light on the fields and stone walls of West Tisbury where the land flattens out below Indian Hill. The proud, venerable white-shingled houses of Edgartown, the silence of an autumn afternoon with the leaves coming down in those narrow, intimate streets. The park at Oak Bluffs with its gazebo in the strangely pearly light, a scene by Seurat. Here the past resonates, some mystery that you can't quite get at. Be absent awhile, and the mystery deepens. The Vineyard recedes like Brigadoon, wrapped in the haze of the smoky southwest wind dashing in over Vineyard Sound.

"It's time you got out in the world again," my family told me before I left the Island. And a good friend, a Vineyarder, advised, "The Island is like a womb to some people. It traps them." And so, dutifully, I left. And broke a promise I'd made to myself, that I'd never live in a city again.

Cautiously, I re-entered the so-called "real world," and before too long it became mine again. The closed, abstracted faces of the crowds on a city street. Carbon monoxide fumes, shimmering up out of stalled logjams of cars at rush hour. The pounding of the jukebox at a local spot, and the sassy broad-shouldered waiters in jeans and white shirts. The winos panhandling on Dupont Circle. National Airport. The Amtrak stations. Baltimore, with its shadeless streets and row houses, the sullen young and tired old slumped on crumbling steps. The students in Charles Village, and their rock music on the first warm days of spring roaring in windows flung wide. The ball park on 33rd Street, fragrant of beer and peanuts. The air in the city smelling of grease and cinders.

A siren shrieked past like a nightmare at midnight, but soon I didn't wake or

Spring planting at Whippoorwill Farm in West Tisbury.

*A grove of fir trees off
Lambert's Cove Road.*

notice. I hardly noticed the crazy man hollering at an imaginary lover at noontime on Connecticut Avenue. Or the tall man who walked solemnly about the Capitol and Old Senate Office Building with a Bible under his arm dressed as Abraham Lincoln. A couple of cops arresting an angry-looking kid for grabbing a purse near the Library of Congress; you walked and didn't look back.

Living on the Island, you become familiar with life's basic chemistries, the flux, the transformations of air and matter. The leaves come down and you let them gather in drifts, till the fall rains press them to a dark, sour mash blanket which settles over the winter, over the years, becomes topsoil. A tree falls on the damp forest floor; quickly, the moisture eats into its marrow, tunneling insects colonize it, and one year it comes apart in weightless red-brown clumps, crumbling, feeding the roots of the ferns. You watch as your compost heap turns black. In your garden you bury a putrid tautog, brought ashore by a November gale, and next summer your tomatoes grow wild and lush over the spot.

When a storm tears an oak out of the ground, harvest it quickly. It is red inside, like a blood-orange. Tap in a wedge. Moisture oozes from the fissure. An oak log two feet in diameter divides with a shudder, after perhaps three well-aimed sledgehammer blows. It splits easily into triangular sections, a blood-orange segment. The color drains away, and the winds playing up off of Vineyard Sound pour through the woodpile, stroking the oak logs to a dry, yellow-gray. Heat, energy: on a winter's night you can sit close to the fire, and lower the thermostat to 50.

In the fall, the wet, sweet-and-sour smell of decay hangs on the cooling air. In spring the breezes dance, and the scents are green, faintly spicy.

I could not pass a fallen tree in Rock Creek Park, or a lightning-blasted trunk turning gray, without sizing it up as firewood. It seemed wrong to throw egg shells and orange peels and good aluminum into a plastic bag. Washington comes alight with azaleas in late April, but unlike my great-grandmother's azalea, which has grown taller than I am, those city azaleas must be fertilized, for no fallen leaves gather to feed their roots.

123

*Twin horses grazing
in a daisy field off
Old County Road.*

Nothing goes back to the earth; garbage, leaves, mown grass is taken away in plastic bags.

The insides of my car windows would become as dirty as the outsides with the sooty film left by the city air. Sometimes in the summer the smog canopy draping Washington became so dense that the morning sun was squeezed to a pink liquid ball in a smoky yellow sky. Living there, they would say, is like smoking a pack of cigarettes a day.

When I left the Vineyard, I did not expect to be away long. But there seemed to be one more task to complete, one more place to go, one more promise to keep. In the meantime, the Vineyard waited. Daydreaming, I rode the back of my friend the south wind, passing over white beaches and green seas till I dismounted in some pretty clearing in North Tisbury.

"What is this tug you feel toward the Vineyard?" asked a good friend of mine, and I wondered how to answer him. I wondered whether I was pulled for the same reasons as the bluejeaned kids who come slouching out of the maw of the Islander, or as the yacht clubbers, the brokers, doctors, celebrities, with their fine houses in Edgartown and seaview homes sprawling on the hills of Seven Gates Farm. Do we all hear the same beckoning call? Hitchhiking down Route 93, or jumping off in a private plane from LaGuardia, do we answer the same summons?

I don't know. My own antecedents on the Vineyard go back four generations. My great-great-grandfather was a Vineyard Haven—then Holmes Hole—whaling captain. My great-grandfather found his summer home in North Tisbury in 1898. In these 90 odd years, the land has become sacred to my family. If the ghosts of my forebears walk, it is in those woods, and glades, and upon those moonlit plank floors. The secret of who I am may be locked up in those wooded hills.

Of course, few among the thousands of us who are pulled toward the Island are joined to it by blood. But perhaps that is beside the point. Perhaps in most people there is an inborn yearning that the Island speaks to, gives promises to. The peace in the empty distances of meadow and stone walls, the gentle towns, the wind in the oaks: all speak a poignant language. There is an innocence here that we all

124

Corn being stored at the Rainbow Farm in Chilmark to be used in winter to feed the animals; 'tis a joy to be simple.

remember, though we may never have known it firsthand. A memory, perhaps, that we are born with.

One day when the southern spring had brought wilting heat and the car and bus fumes hung trapped in the heavy, humid air, I thought: Why not? The river creaked along mud-brown, dirty, while in North Tisbury, I knew, the forsythia had shot their sprangling plumes, and my great-grandmother's azalea was budding. Why not? I thought. I'd been enough places, kept enough promises. Why not? I thought, and suddenly couldn't find an answer.

And so with half my life still before me, I came home.

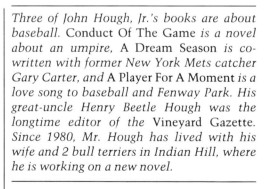

Three of John Hough, Jr.'s books are about baseball. Conduct Of The Game *is a novel about an umpire,* A Dream Season *is co-written with former New York Mets catcher Gary Carter, and* A Player For A Moment *is a love song to baseball and Fenway Park. His great-uncle Henry Beetle Hough was the longtime editor of the* Vineyard Gazette. *Since 1980, Mr. Hough has lived with his wife and 2 bull terriers in Indian Hill, where he is working on a new novel.*

John Hough, Jr., back home.

A confrontation on the seventh hole at Farm Neck.

Vineyard Golf—
A Love Story

BY JIM KAPLAN

olf, Mark Twain once wrote, is a good walk spoiled. Twain never played on Martha's Vineyard, where a round of golf is a good walk enhanced. On a routine day at the Farm Neck course, I have seen swans on the lake behind the fourth green, Canada geese on the seventh hole, osprey near the eighth, red-winged blackbirds on the ninth, a cat and a pheasant on the tenth, a skunk on the eleventh, more geese on the twelfth, two whole geese families on the fifteenth, three French hens, two turtle doves, and a partridge in the pro shop.

There's nothing quite like Vineyard-variety golf, and nature is only part of the story. For one thing, I've played barefoot here; most places don't allow that. For another, I've golfed with the kind of notables who congregate on the Island.

There was the late Yip Harburg, who wrote the lyrics for "Finian's Rainbow" and "The Wizard of Oz." Never was a golfer more appropriately named: Yip had the "yips," a kind of nervous tick golfers get on the green. In fact, he was the worst putter I ever saw.

On another occasion I played with author John Updike. Though wild off the tee, he managed to shoot an 88. Nonetheless, Updike insisted his game always falls apart on the thirteenth or fourteenth hole. "I'm distracted," he said, "by visions of drinks on the veranda."

I especially enjoy a round with my friend Porfirio Foolish, a deposed dictator who mistook Martha's Vineyard for Elba. Porfirio wears a wig to avoid detection, uses security guards as caddies, and falls into Vineyard Sound on every follow-through.

Action on the fourth green at Farm Neck, a nasty little hole.

John Updike walking to his ball on the second fairway at Mink Meadows.

Canada Geese making themselves at home on the eighteenth green at Farm Neck, reason enough to deduct two strokes from the total score.

Most often I've played with yet another species of *golfer vinyardensis*, my parents Ben and Felicia. Celebrated at the nine-hole Mink Meadows course for their speed, they've passed the same golfer twice in one eighteen-hole round. They raised me on those sacred acres, taught me about honors there. I also learned about success and achievement, for it was decreed: one Dairy Queen cone for every par. When I sank a par putt, I salivated over soft ice cream and hard butterscotch sauce. I can still remember that sweet, succulent taste, augmenting the afternoon.

Before she gave up the game for health reasons, my mother swung a mean club. I still hack around with my father. He's a judge, so when he wins a hole, I say, "Your honor, Your Honor." His game is, well, unique. Having never taken lessons, he has a backswing as sweeping as an ant's. He doesn't drive a car, but he does drive golf carts. One afternoon he was motoring toward the fourth tee with a frequent partner when the cart overturned on them. They pulled themselves out, dusted themselves off, and never again spoke of the matter. My parents refer to Mink Meadows as "Minks Links." You just find me a more inventive calling card.

•

There are three Island courses—the 9-hole Edgartown Golf Club, the aforementioned Mink Meadows Golf Course, in West Chop, and the 18-hole Farm Neck Golf Club, in Oak Bluffs.

An Edgartown member told me I could play at his private links as long as I didn't write about the place. I declined to do either.

Mink Meadows, a comely public course, was opened by Robert Bigelow in 1936. Oval-shaped Minks Links has changed little since its inception, although five new traps have been installed and six new tees established to create some variance for people playing a second nine. There's still an excellent view of the Sound from the third and eighth fairways, an occasional deer or quail on the premises, and a wide-open look to the course.

Nature helps make it both challenging and beatable: The wind is usually against golfers on three of the four short par-4's and with them on the two long ones.

"Not all of our golfers are hard-core," says director emeritus Gardner Drew. "It's a gentle course for people who want to relax and play the best golf they can." The regulars, mostly native Islanders, are nothing if not loyal. The clubhouse closes from October 31 until April 15, but you'll see golfers out there all winter, hitting colored balls in the snow.

By contrast, semi-public Farm Neck has undergone many a transformation. First built around the turn of the century, it has variously been known as the Oak Bluffs Country Club, the Island Country Club, and no club when bankruptcy closed it briefly in the 1970's.

In 1976-7 Geoff Cornish and Bill Robinson laid out and opened a new front nine for the soon-to-be-bankrupt owners. "Donald Ross, the grand master of golf architects, said 'God creates golf holes in New England; it's a golf architect's duty to find them,'" reports Cornish. He and Robinson discovered a short, tight, exacting nine with many traps and trees, two challenging carries over water, and a lush, Augusta-style feeling to parts of it.

In 1978 the Farm Neck Association bought a 500-acre parcel including the course and assigned the design of the back side to Patrick Mulligan. Holes 10-18 opened in 1979. Longer and more open than the front nine, they're a bit reminiscent of the Scottish seaside courses where the pros play the British Open. The 12th hole, a dogleg with a pond that restricts the tee-off and guards the green, is Farm Neck's finest.

"We've been tinkering, adding some traps on the back nine, and the two sides are starting to meld," says general manager Tim Sweet. What also unites the course is the sight of old farm equipment scattered about the property. Parts of Farm Neck look as if they were designed by Andrew Wyeth.

Of late the course has become as trendy as a Wyeth exhibit. Professionals like Orville Moody and Doug Sanders drop by for the Martha's Vineyard Hospital

Pro-Am, high-rollers from off-Island tour the links in carts, and the 18-hole rates range from $20 to $50, depending on the time of year. Club members are eligible for cheaper rates, handicap service, tournaments, and preferred tee times. There's a waiting list for membership. I've already been on it for several years.

With ever-increasing demand, the Island needs a third public course. Some golf mavens say the land behind the skating rink in Oak Bluffs is a likely site, but the Vineyard entered the 1990's amid debate over who owned it. So don't hold your breath. Just hold your score down.

•

A hardy breed of winter golfers stalk the Island courses come rain, hail, ice, sleet, or snow.

The golf holes that most intrigue me are those that teach me something about myself.

When I arrive at Mink Meadows' fifth hole, I usually harbor hopes for a good round. The par-3 fifth will determine if I get one. It's only 163 yards, and the temptation is to go right for the flag. But five is a tricky little hole: uphill, with sidehill bounces kicking the ball to the trap and gully on the left or into the woods or next tee on the right. And anyone reaching the small green on the fly risks careening into a trap or trees.

When I was younger, I invariably took out a long iron and swung away. The result was often short and disastrous. With the benefit of maturity, I began pulling out a 5-wood and found I could easily reach the green. Or, alas, the woods. Double bogeys usually followed.

Is there no way to play this hole? One day, in a flash of insight, I pulled out a 6-iron and pitched to a relatively flat landing area some 10 yards short of the green. Then I chipped on and canned the par putt. Better scoring through safety: a lesson of middle age.

My favorite at Farm Neck is the seventh. There's no more beautiful sight in golf than a ball carrying over water, and there's virtually no way to reach the seventh green other than a pitch over the pond. It makes or breaks my round; it's my watershed or Waterloo.

In years past I'd pull out an iron and feel my knees shaking. "Got to clear that pond," I'd think. With a ferocious swing, I'd fall back on my right foot and dribble the ball into the water. Round closed. Later I learned I could hit the ball farther by swinging easier, with a natural transfer of weight from right to left. The Rolling Stones were wrong: What a drag it *isn't* growing old.

•

Vineyard golf is the love of my summer and, fittingly enough, a motif in the love of my life. My wife Brooks and I had our first date at Farm Neck. The front nine passed without incident. On the eleventh tee the true confessions began. By fourteen we were talking so earnestly and golfing so slowly that a sixsome played through us.

Three years after I lost my heart at Farm Neck, I lost my wedding ring there, too. When golfing, I used to switch the ring from my left hand to my overlapping right pinky to keep from squeezing it against the club shaft. One day we were playing in the rain, and I kept drying my wet hand on my trousers. Over post-round drinks, I looked at my hand. It was bare: despair!

Next morning we took an electric cart and retraced the previous day's round. It's amazing what you can find when you're looking at the ground. I once discovered two $100 bills on New York's East Side; this time we were looking for something you can't put a price on. We found plenty—a pair of sunglasses, two new golf balls, a few dozen unbroken tees, hundreds of cigarette butts, some goose feathers—but no ring.

The twelfth hole at Farm Neck can quickly turn a good round into a disaster.

As we made our way across the course, we stopped foursome after foursome to explain our plight and ask them to keep an eye out. "Needle in a haystack," people moaned, promising nonetheless to look hard. The pros, maintenance and restaurant personnel couldn't have been nicer. As we sped along, I had an epiphany: all of Farm Neck, united, thinking of my welfare! Just to be sure, I posted a reward of $50.

That afternoon a man called us. He had found the ring on the eighteenth tee. We raced over to his house, and there it was. "Now," he said, turning to his wife as he pocketed the reward, "you can buy me a case of Guinness Stout."

•

Missing wedding rings are the least of Vineyard golf's current problems. We used to be able to walk onto a course and play. The links are so crowded these days that golfers need to call ahead for tee-off times and risk being paired with strangers in polka-dot pants and Hawaiian shirts. Mink Meadows has acquired advertisement-covered tee markers and a ranger who patrols the fairways urging faster play. Vineyard courses now frown on barefoot players (Hint: Remove your shoes on the second tee). Worst of all, polite golfers are becoming an endangered species. More and more I'm seeing guys in their early 20's with little mustaches and fraternity-house beer bellies, playing out of automatic carts and yelling to each other as they whack balls over my head or cut in front of me without asking.

•

One afternoon I was playing a round with my friend Miles Jaffee, an excellent sailor, skier, and tennis player who never bothered to master golf. After one particularly bad shot—history will record it occurring on the fourth hole at Minks Links—Miles picked up his ball and threw it toward the hole. His eyes lit up: The thrill of invention was about to replace the agony of defeat. Miles put away his clubs and played several holes using throws only. If his score didn't improve, his mood certainly did.

Taking Miles's lead, I herewith offer some inventions of my own for improving Vineyard golf:

- Permit one throw per round in place of a shot. As I write, I'm thinking about that nasty sand trap in front of the fifth green at Minks Links.
- Allow five shots per round to be replayed (Farm Neck has a tournament based on this idea). Think of the putts you've missed, the shots you've plunked into the water or woods. This country was founded on the premise of a second chance; golf should be, too.

This innovation, of course, doesn't count the customary first-tee mulligan. That's a right, not a privilege.

- If you haven't warmed up on the putting green, putt two balls on the first green and count the better one. Also, count no more than three putts on the green and concede any close enough to the hole to measure inside the grip of your putter. There's no reason to contract a case of Yip's "yips."
- Always play preferred lies on the fairway. Not the rough, though. I do have a few standards.
- Never count more than seven strokes for a hole. That's the rule in miniature golf; why not the big game?

Back when he still counted strokes, my father used to announce his score, followed by the palliative "with some allowances." Well, why not? Put a little more fun into it, and Vineyard golf could be the best walk Mark Twain never had.

A summer resident of Chilmark and Oak Bluffs, Jim Kaplan is editor of Baseball Research Journal, *a former staff writer for* Sports Illustrated, *and the author of five books about baseball.*

A scenic situation at Zack's Cliffs.

Observations On A Nude Beach

BY RICHARD LOURIE

To enter the parking lot for Lucy Vincent Beach (half nude, half regular), on Martha's Vineyard, you must have the requisite sticker on your car. The sticker is cheap. But to obtain the sticker from town hall, you must be a resident or be able to prove that you are a summer renter. And summer rentals are very expensive. And so the invisible shaping power of money is at work even on the idyllic stretch of sand where people shed clothes and neuroses, and life becomes as simple as the sky. Or to put it another way, the poor are not only ill-clothed, they can't even afford to be naked.

•

No matter what the winter storms do to the contours of the shore, the beach is the one place that always seems exactly the same, just as it was in childhood, when your grandparents were alive and laughing, and you could rest your head against the side of your mother's leg as if it were a hill.

•

In the beginning, at least, the beauty of the beach offers a stern challenge to the life I have been leading up to the moment when, barefoot at the edge of the water, I stop and look out at the ocean for the first time that summer.

The challenge is very simple. It says: you have a certain amount of time. To some degree you are free to spend that time as you think best. What is the best way to spend it? Smoking, sipping coffee, hunched over a keyboard, playing endlessly with the 26 letters of the English alphabet? Or living a life that always has the feeling of being outdoors?

But the challenge does not come from the beauty of the beach; it comes from me. I'm the one who's always pestering myself with questions. And I've got plenty of answers, too. It's just that I don't find any of them ultimately acceptable. I'm too familiar with their source.

•

We're Americans and we like changes and we like them quick. Still sometimes it's amazing how quickly we change. Thirty years ago vegetarianism, nudism, yogurt, and yoga were only for nature boys and weirdoes. Now they've become fixtures, businesses, passé.

America loves variety, the spice of life; America loves fun. There are fun ways to make money if you're smart, and fun itself is a business. People who invent a really good new way to have fun in America will make plenty of money and have plenty of time to loll about nude beaches, unless, of course, their success has also infected them with the disease of ambition. Then they will not be truly relaxing but restoring themselves for new achievements, which is not at all the same thing. There're always a few of them jogging doggedly by the edge of the water.

•

Every place has its nature and its strict, unwritten rules. The rules of the nude beach are the opposite of the street's. On the street you do not look into an approaching stranger's eyes. On the nude beach you are supposed to look *only* into a stranger's eyes.

Another reversal: at the nude beach men's usual fear of not getting an erection becomes the fear of getting one.

•

To be naked and to take one's clothes off are not the same thing. Some people shed their social self as if it were a T-shirt that they could just pull up and off. But

Up, up and away.

133

The family that bathes together stays together.

Beauty and the Beast.

others are so convinced of their own importance that they cannot leave their social self home for even an afternoon. Here comes a nationally known figure, naked as the day he was born, and yet he seems to be striding into a T.V. studio for his daily talk show program.

•

The human body is so plain, it needs all the art it can get. Naked, we are mostly comical and even a bit dreary, the ginks of nature.

Sex and art have been closely related since the start of civilization. The eternal games of peek-a-boo and hide-and-seek can be played with bits of bark and grass or cleverly cut pieces of cloth from Bloomingdale's. It's a short distance from a painter slashing a red streak across his canvas to a woman applying her lipstick.

•

There are certain things that automatically make you feel happier and freer—riding in the back of an open truck is one. Rolling in the mud is another, at least for some people. Wallowing in the mud and clay at the base of the seaside cliffs, basting themselves with it, sculpting themselves with it into laughing aborigines from the pages of the *National Geographic*.

Why do they do it? I wonder. Is it because of all those times that their mothers called from the door not to come home a dirty mess? Is it because the buildup of clay creates a new body, a new physical feel that is an even rarer sensation than being naked in public? Or is some Freudian contraption of a theory required here? Or could rolling in the mud be apart of our true nature that takes years of constant civilizing to shame us out of? Or is it just plain slippery eroticism?

There's only one way to find out.

•

The little clumps and tribes we form on the beach are a sociology in themselves. When we went to Salisbury Beach in the now unimaginable forties, we went as three whole families, unless people were visiting, as they usually were, and then our clan was all the greater. I never see that now. But maybe I don't go to the right beaches. People who go to nude beaches never seem to have more than 1.3 children. And the people with 5,6,7 would never be caught dead on a nude beach. Why?

A dedicated follower of fashion.

Lounging in clay—a favorite Vineyard pastime.

Cosmic jump.

The nude beach is a chaste place. Still, lust always enjoys appearing at improbable moments. It has come upon me while riding in the back of an ambulance, helping a nurse keep someone alive. (The lust was for the nurse, not the victim.) And someone once told me that she fell in love with a neighbor while warning him that their building was on fire. So if these two incidents can happen, we are not safe anywhere.

•

Overheard: "My agent is trying to package the concept before I start on the script," says a well-greased young man with sunglasses, turning onto his stomach."

"I'm really excited for you," says the woman producer sitting besides him. "I'd love to see the script when it's written."

Not before?

•

When the little children come running by naked, they don't seem naked. Not like we do.

•

Binoculars and cameras are unwelcome at the nude beach. People dress to be looked at in public but do not want to be looked at when they undress in public. People want to lose themselves in the dream of freedom, freedom from society and its restrictive clothing. Feet hate shoes. But a camera can break that spell, as when you are lost in a book and you feel a stranger's glance on the side of your face.

•

I can recall being mildly shocked to realize that women had rib cages and were not composed entirely of magical sexual flesh.

•

It is absolutely impossible for people just to walk and sit on sand. They have to let it run through their fingers, throw it at each other, bury each other in it, build castles out of it, dig holes in it until water is reached or the sides keep caving in. People cannot resist the urge to collect and to decorate. Some look for shells, some for colored pebbles and sea glass, while others are interested solely in gull

A pick-up game at Lucy Vincent Beach.

Near the end of a glorious day.

Friendly competition.

Decent exposures at Windy Gates.

feathers. Shells and sticks are laid out in patterns. Odd little shrines are made. Art that lasts for only a day, like those insects that are born in the morning and die in the evening.

●

One of the things the beach gives back to us is the sky. We are more aware of the sky as children; adulthood is a city, busy, dense, and crowded. In Manhattan the sky seems like an afterthought. After all, there had to be a little coloration between the tops of buildings.

●

For some people the beach is a quiet religion. And they feel more mystery in the endless youth of the waves than in any ancient cathedral.

Every so often on that beach there is a woman who spellbinds me. One year it was a woman who was there with her husband and two children. But the fact that she was a married mother had no relevance to me, because my adoration was free of any conniving. Even my conscience was willing to believe that I was not even preparing fantasy plans for covert action, and so it did not excrete any of its poisonous juices into my bloodstream. A rare moment of freedom.

I somehow felt that this woman lived a life where love had a large place, as it really does not in most lives. Hers was a strong, serene, and happy love, and her face, her arms, and even her back radiated a golden sexual health. At that moment I wanted to be with her, know who she was, hear her voice speaking to me for the rest of my life.

But then I got thirsty and rolled over for a cold drink.

●

Sometimes the tense barrier of self-consciousness melts away in the heat and safety of the beach and you are just simply there, like a piece of driftwood on which a hat has been tossed.

●

The beach is spotted with nipples, dark against the lighter bodies, like the markings on a giraffe. Human beings have argued for centuries whether we are animals or higher forms. But the two nip-

139

A view from South Mountain looking East to the extremity of Lucy Vincent Beach and beyond.

ples on every person state simply that we are mammals. Warm-blooded, born in a certain way, suckling the young. But mammals with the gift of speech, building and destroying wherever we go. Mammals that keep museums and fly into space.

•

The exact difference between pleasure and pain can be measured in the speed of the offshore breeze. At one speed the breeze is like pure song playing over our bodies. If it moves just a little faster, it begins to lash sand against our bodies as if we were aging buildings being sandblasted as part of an urban renewal plan.

•

Islandness. The feeling of returning to the mainland after a summer on the Island is like going from weightlessness to gravity. But, fortunately or unfortunately, we cannot remember much of the Island feeling during the winter, and in summer the memory of snow and overcoats vanishes like yesterday's hangover. The only thing the human memory seems particularly adept at recalling is miniscule slights from the distant past.

•

Many of the people who frequent nude beaches in New England are avid readers. Some of them are addicted to reading and would start to feel vaguely edgy if they went without reading matter for a few days.

Some of them read books that require mental effort. Perhaps they've just started on their vacation and still have not fully surrendered their winter lives. I once saw a New York psychiatrist so involved in *Ego, Hunger and Aggression* that he failed to notice that his three-year-old daughter had fallen off her inflatable raft and had begun to drown. Fortunately not everyone was busy honing their intellects at that moment.

Some people read new hardbacks, the pattern of covers reproducing *The New York Times* best-seller-list against a background of dunes and umbrellas.

Summer is when we allow ourselves to read for pleasure. In winter we read mostly to further us in our professions and to fall asleep. But in the summertime, sophisticated women shamelessly devour fat paperback romances, and noted intellectuals devour mysteries like potato chips.

Perhaps the books people read on the beach are only worry beads for the mind. To keep the mind busy so that it will not plague us like a hyperactive child.

But it's difficult to read on the beach. The white pages become a dazzling mirror. Sweat runs into your eyes, blurring the black lines of print like the mascara of a woman who has been crying.

And then you are ready for the real reason you came there—the waves.

•

Bodysurfing naked is one of life's great elations. But, as with many other pleasures, there is a certain trick involved, a knack. The trick is to know which waves are worth riding, and to be able to catch them at the moment just before they begin to break so that you are lifted and then propelled like a torpedo toward shore. This is the moment just before the wave "breaks its wrists." That's the problem—how can you tell when it's the moment just before? It's like asking directions on the subway and being told by someone to get off one station before he does.

But actually it's simple. All you have to do is pay attention to the waves. They are nearly always what they appear to be. Simple as dogs. Though some do have quirks and even a mean side.

Some waves will deceive you—like a bull catching a matador on its horns. In California, where I used to live, the surfers call one especially mean type of wave a "washing machine" because of the way it tumbles you around. Like the Eskimo with their 12 basic words for snow, the surfers have a vast and detailed knowledge of the waves, which gives them a great freedom in the water. Dreaded riptides are just a quick escalator for them, and they can tell within a few yards just how far out they'll be taken. But the surfers' favorite sea is a stormy midnight one, with sheet lightning and wild waves. Then they get drunk and take LSD and paddle out to the great swells and ride them in, howling with victory and insanity—Vikings entering Valhalla.

Some waves are like dolphins and the ride they give you is fast, strong, and friendly. But the ideal wave causes a little fear and awe as it rises mighty as a whale. The tingle of healthy fear is part of the thrill. No mistakes can be made when riding those waves. And if one is made, you have to know what to do and what to avoid doing when you are the helpless spinning prisoner of three tons of water on the move. The main thing is, don't fight—for the simple reason that you'll lose. But at the same time, you can't let the wave start bending you like a twig that could snap. These waves are not recommended for beginners.

I look down the water. The waves are long. I cannot see even the faces of the people who will ride the wave with me.

Forty, maybe 50, men, women, and children are bobbing in the water, watching with amused disdain as some are lured by disappointing waves that lose their vim after 15 feet or so. But then a great wave begins to rise. A surge of excitement runs through everybody, so strong and clear that we can feel it in one another. There is one second left to duck under the wave and then that second is gone. I hear whoops of glee and exhilaration as the wave force comes around me, takes me, and hurls me toward the waves' eternal destination, the shore.

Then fighting my way back out for more and more, I can feel a vital wildness in me and hear the talk show of my mind go off the air. The sun is golden, the sky is clear, the charged brine of the Atlantic has brought me back to my senses, and everywhere I look there is only life and the beauty of life.

"I'm sure mine will be an Aquarius. . . . and yours?"

Richard Lourie was born and raised in Boston, and has devoted much of his professional career to Russia. He has translated over thirty books from Russian and Polish to English. He is the author of four books, including the critically acclaimed novel, Zero Gravity *(Harcourt Brace and Javonovitch). He freelances for various publications including* Boston Magazine, The New York Times, The Washington Post *and* New Republic. *He is occasionally seen without clothes on Lucy Vincent Beach, incognito of course.*

Moonrise at the terminal building in Oak Bluffs.

The Golden Goose Goes Honkey Tonk

BY JAY SAPIR

"Everybody wants to be the last one off the boat."
—Former Oak Bluffs Selectman Anthony "Tubby" Rebello

★ ★ ★

"To me, 'honkey tonk' just means the fun place to go."
— Former Oak Bluffs Selectman Ed Coogan

It was October, 1989. A coup attempt took place in Panama, and thus more work for me. Loyalist troops were scrubbing down the bullet marks from the fortress of Manuel Noriega, the day after rebel soldiers failed to overthrow the dictator. The General was plotting revenge. The rebels were praying for their hides. And I am thinking about Developments of Regional Impact.

"D.R.I.'s" Ah, the way they settled spats on the Vineyard: If some territorial squabble got too hot for one town to handle—throw it to the Martha's Vineyard Commission. They would give thumbs up or down to the D.R.I. The only violence would be the unbridled invective of the pro- or anti-development forces. Bloodless coups were the order of the day.

Where was the Panama City Commission when we needed them? What this town needs is a strong dose of New England style democracy. Maybe the citizens could have a town meeting and put the General's tenure on a "warrant article."

The truth is, once the Vineyard gets inside your skin, you're a goner for life. A lifer sentenced to a grand, serene vision of what you would like the planet to be.

Martha's Vineyard is a glimmering little jewel that infects your psyche.

Through many long winters, the Vineyard was my beat and covering it was often an act of unrequited love. Toward the end, I saw the Island as a sophisticated banana republic whose banana was the tourist trade. But now, looking out over the charred aftermath of a bloody coup, I realize that the comparison is odious. Life is much nastier on the General's turf where one gang of armed thugs controls all the bananas.

Oh to be back in Menemsha on a sun-soaked day: where the only dictator is zoning law; the only bombing comes from Nomans Land, where rare birds and bombing targets live side by side. Now, there's a Development of Regional Impact—for the birds anyway.

It's tougher to get a good paying job in the streets of Panama City, than getting a business permit in Menemsha. Although both are fishing towns near bombing ranges.

It would be tempting to think of the Vineyard as some kind of ideal place upon which to plant a picture-postcard view of the world. But as I recall the reality of the day to day Island life, I realize nothing could be farther from the truth.

And as I gaze upon the bullet scarred walls of Panama's military compound, visions of the Vineyard tease my mind. I've been reporting the Noriega coup for two

The East Chop lighthouse.

and popcorn perking from nearby Circuit Avenue. A breeze ripe with Island smells that rattled fuel barrels aboard fishing boats and blew puffs of barbecue smoke on shore from yachts.

The breeze drifted by ghosts of porch lanterns not yet lit for the soon to be celebrated Illumination Night. The night that Methodist settlers set aside for pre-revival revelry. A night to lite up beside the glow of Chinese lanterns—rumored to have come from whaling ships in from the Orient. A night of lamp-lit parades when the first fireworks were fired over Ocean Park.

A night that dates back to a time when the rest of the Nation could be in Civil War, but revivals and soul-searching Illuminations came first.

Inside Oak Bluffs town hall a war of words was being fought in ways never imagined by The Founders. The feud did have a revival flavor only because it was revived every summer. Citizens and elected officials were fighting over how many ferries the Steamship Authority had decided to route their way.

Some merchants were screaming they had been robbed by the fast talkers of Tisbury who used their clout to steer more boats into Vineyard Haven Harbor. There were accusations and allegations. Conflicts of interest or just interesting conflicts? Who knows, but business was being lost.

Then one elderly fisherman-turned-plumber rose to speak his piece. The Island had been tragically transformed in his weather battered eyes. Gone were days of crystal scallop beds in West Tisbury. The carefree clamming "down-Island" had been displaced by a season of endless permits: permits for "commercial" and permits for "family," for residents and non residents. Fees and licenses and permits negotiated through a Harbor Constable. At the behest of the Shellfish Advisory Committee. Answerable to the honorable Board of Selectman, acting on advice from the Harbor Advisory Committee. Multiplied by the six Island towns.

Worse. The languid harbor graced by wooden scallop boats, come summer

nights without sleep and the fortress walls are starting to dissolve. Like an old sweet song, a dream-like vision of the Island comes into play.

Let us go then back to one sultry summer night when a gloating August moon bathed Oak Bluffs Harbor in a dreamy golden light.

A precious night when the gentlest harbor breeze cooled the winding back streets of old Cottage City. A breeze blowing in from East Chop reeking of salt from the sea and sweat from the swimmers. The breeze swept through the campground gingerbread cottages redolent with lily blossoms, gin and tonics,

turned into a floating carnival. Gaudy ferries fat with tourists carried a new breed of "off-Islander." The ones who came only in summer and roamed Main Street, Tisbury or Edgartown, or Circuit Avenue, with dollar signs for eyes. Then after "skimming the cream" off the Island economy, they would pack up and go back to their real off-Island homes somewhere.

"What will we do," the old Portuguese fisherman asked, "when we kill the goose that laid the golden egg?"

Silence fell on the town hall meeting for it was a question which haunted all six Vineyard towns.

The tour buses were strangling the Gay Head Cliffs. The barrier beaches of Chilmark were being flooded by naked hippies. Alley's General Store in West Tisbury got so busy they had to build a new addition. Developers had torn up Edgartown with houses on quarter acre lots. But if you went up-Island to Gay Head or Chilmark, you had to buy two to three acres on which to build a home. Who could afford that on an Island paycheck alone?

Who was murdering the golden goose?

The question that haunted the Island had special meaning for Oak Bluffs.

Indeed, time had not been altogether kind to old "Cottage City." The young summer throngs saw the Bluffs as the sandy path to fast kicks, easy romance, and loud all-night parties. Along with Edgartown, it's the Island's other "wet town," and on any summer night Circuit Avenue became Circus Avenue. A funky parade of sun stroked mooners, beach babes and bar boys, BMW's and bikers buzzing cramped streets drowned by the roar of moped motors. Mopeders, bicycles, guys on the make and girls on the fast track; a sticky sea of humanity looking for kicks beneath the ghosts of porch lamps not yet lit, down streets whose lamps await the night of Illumination.

Just gaze out the windows of the historic Wesley House. Slip upon slip of yachts and pleasure boats stare back at you.

"One of these days," the old Portuguese fisherman warned, "we're gonna kill the

Oak Bluffs harbor bustling in mid-summer.

Part of the Tabernacle, the spiritual center of Oak Bluffs.

145

goose that laid the golden egg. Then what'll we do?"

"Maybe then, no one will come here anymore," finally came the reply from the back of the hall.

There were nights on end of arguments like this. One popular Selectman spent a whole summer living down a remark about Oak Bluffs having become the Island's "Honkey Tonk" town. For there were differing definitions of Honkey Tonk in the minds of those who lived and worked in what used to be called Cottage City.

Was Honkey Tonk a fatal sign that the graceful old past was gone for good? Or did Honkey Tonk simply mean a place to go for a night of celebration. Wasn't that the intent of Illumination Night? Surely there was a strong case to be made for big fun to be had in Oak Bluffs. The Sea View Hotel was proof of that.

Here was a fading, weather beaten old beauty proudly planted in front of the town beach. A Tennessee Williams stage set for nightly musical-comedy. And always presided over by the indomitable Loretta: An eccentric woman of saintly compassion cleverly disguised as a tough talking bar matron. The bar's shuttered windows looked out over a sparkling sea. Its fading mahogany bar the raw canvas for the lost genius of Johnny the bartender-gambler-horseman-philosopher-extraordinaire.

Intense action at the Flying Horses *carousel, the nation's oldest, in Oak Bluffs.*

The Johnny and Loretta show rocked the Sea View every night along with jazz, rock, and blues bands culled from the Island's home grown talent. On rare nights, Loretta would join the band for a chorus of "My Blue Heaven" or her favorite "Ukulele Lady."

"If you love Ukulele Lady, Ukulele Lady loves you!" And everyone in the house loved the "Ukulele Lady"—at least until closing time when Loretta picked up her vintage plastic billy club and gave the hangers on a sound mock thrashing.

The grand old Sea View Hotel with its sweeping balustrades, wooden dance floor, and seaside balconies. All gone now. A condominium largely unsold in its place.

Yet Oak Bluffs was always a hustling town swaggering down the road to merriment, from pre-pilgrim days when Capawock Tribesmen were kidnapped by English explorers hustling Sassafras Root to cure the plagues of Europe. A jaunty town by the sea where Methodist ministers built the sprawling campground Tabernacle and converted all who'd listen: Black, Indian and White. A faraway harbor town that made a dizzying descent into commerce's grip.

Across the street from where shiploads of zealots built a crazy quilt of surreal cottages, the harbor strip now stands. A mini-mall mixed with fried clams, topical art, and T-shirt shops. Cross the street to the Circuit Avenue strip where glazed eye kids gobble pizza under the mystical eyes of "The Flying Horses"—the nation's oldest carousel. A candy colored merry-go-round spinning at the edge of history.

And this is what irked the old fisherman. Scallop ponds were fast polluting or overfished. Year-round working people couldn't find year-round housing. A lot of families had to move twice a year when seasonal rentals skyrocketed. The hordes poured off the Ferries to geek at the gingerbread houses, roast on the beach, get a quick fix of fun and go home. What had become of old Cottage City?

What we now know as Oak Bluffs was "founded" by the Methodists in 1835 as

the Weslyan Grove Camp Meeting. What they "found" there were Indians on what they called the Isle of Nope. Indians who did not share their agenda. Tribes whose allegiance was to Massasoit, Great Sachem of the Wampanoags, Takemmies, Chappaquiddicks, and Capawocks.

But by 1865—historians tell us—the settlement was becoming famous for its maze of sleek angular cottages and seaside groves.

In 1867, writes Ellen Weiss in her "City in the Woods," the "planned resort" of Oak Bluffs was laid out next to the Weslyan Grove Camp Meeting Grounds. By then, partying was becoming an art form.

Weiss writes of a Boston journalist who observed an Illumination Night tradition called "The Antiques and Horribles" parade. It resembled a Mardi Gras parade led by a "tin pan drum corps, followed by ghosts yielding croquet mallets, Chinese and Japanese figures, Siamese Twins, indescribable things and a satanic majesty. A comet, a Brigham Young and a walking caricature of poor Nancy Luce. Miss Luce was a particularly deranged Island woman who sold to tourists copies of her love poems made for her pet chickens."

The Illumination Night madness was a wild prelude to the weekend revival meeting. Weiss observes that by 1870 Oak Bluffs was seen as an "ideal city with magical overtones. A city of the imagination, a work of art . . . (the cottages) constitute an independent American building type, probably invented at this site by local carpenters. These cottages sit cheek by jowl on tiny lots that leave no room for private lawns. Outdoor space is communal; grand and little parks and avenues in a jumbled relationship."

So Oak Bluffs grew up around the mystical maze of cottage-lined streets, built on Indian land for communal soul cleansing. It was, quite literally destined to become a resort. And what a resort it has become. None who planned it could have imagined the Circuit Avenue strip jutting quite so close to the residential back streets of the old campground. Close enough for porch dwellers to throw stones at bar stools. So close in fact that truckers hauling beer and wine (I used to be one) had to drape cloths over the booze boxes on their flatbeds so campground sensibilities would not be upset. Although nightfall would bring the smell of hot rum toddies from the pastel porches

Heavy snow warnings at Sengekontacket.

The patterns of winter.

of the self-righteous.

Oak Bluffs is not so much a case of a town that has fallen from grace—more a matter of a town where fun and grace grew up in close proximity.

Just like the Vineyard itself only more so.

And the Vineyard—as a place for fun and grace—is a humble sample of the best civilization has to offer. Just like the nation but more so.

And the nation has certainly had its struggles to regulate fun along side of grace. Some have called that "trying to legislate morality." Just like the rest of the Planet—and sometimes, more so!

What is it after all that they are arguing about in all those town halls for all those years?

They are fighting for the right to have fun and not destroy the grace that has bought them there.

As far as political arguments go, this one is surely being fought on the high ground. But it all comes back, as if in a dream, when I wander the back streets of Panama City, on a day when fighting for fun is unheard of in the fight to survive. What a way to settle an argument.

That little jewel that infects you for life.

Few tourists get to see the famous "Pink House" during this time of year.

Closed for the season.

149

The Gazebo at dusk.

Gingerbread fairyland.

For years I faithfully covered news of great consequence on Martha's Vineyard. I would drive my old clunker or thumb a ride through snow storms to listen to hours of debate on whether to build a new school annex or fix up the old one. What color and decor should the rest rooms be? Maybe the town should triple the "transient vendor's fee," so Tisbury's summer skimmers would have less profits to skim. When is Upper Main Street in Edgartown going to grow into Main Drag, Cape Cod? Should we freeze growth? What would happen to the building trades? What would happen to people who need homes?

Everywhere I go these days somebody is proclaiming a new doctrine. The Russians have replaced the "Brezhnev" doctrine with the "Sinatra" doctrine that lets east bloc countries "do it their way." Central America is said to be still under the influence of "The Reagan Doctrine," so we have to pay for guns to El Salvador. The European Community is reported to be rejecting the "Thatcher Doctrine."

On Martha's Vineyard, life was run according to the Tubby Rebello Doctrine.

Actually it wasn't the former Selectman who coined the phrase or first thought the thought. Maybe it wasn't even an Islander. But whoever said it said it right: "Everybody wants to be the last one off the boat."

The last one off has the right to turn around and say who else can come. The last one off the boat gets the last liquor pouring license in Edgartown. The last car gets the last "guaranteed standby" space. The last guy who owns his strip of beach is the last guy that's going to have one. The last lady gets the last dance in the last night club.

The last dictator gets the last of the guns. Anyone else that tries to get off the boat gets shot.

The stakes may be higher in Panama, but the passion runs as deep in Gay Head. Just try and build a barn without a building permit. Or tack up some shingles that don't meet the color code. You might be able to wrangle a "variance," but it probably went to the last guy off the boat.

Trying to get to the bottom of a story on the Vineyard was like walking through a minefield, only the mines were boards and commissions. Boards of zoning and boards of planning. Appeals boards and boards of trustees. Library boards and school boards, Police and Fire commissioners, county commissioners, Martha's Vineyard Commissioners, shellfish committees, harbor advisory committees, parks committees, finance committees, and special ad hoc committees.

You could spend a whole summer arguing over the last moped rental license in Oak Bluffs.

But who could argue with the enduring wisdom of a salty town whose blue-green seascape glowed in wooden porch windows on that golden summer night. A sea town of soul people. Methodist ministers and all-night madmen. Parishioners and partyers. A town whose rambling homes and churches spoke of dignity and the time when revelation figured into architecture.

A town of fun-seeking devils and honkey tonk angels cruising streets built by Christian virtue.

A lusty labyrinth of sea-swept light flooding the lamps of Illumination Night.

Jay Sapir gained his foothold in broadcast journalism while News Director for WMVY, the Island radio station. After being News Director for a National Public Radio affiliate in Alaska, he became a Washington correspondent/editor for the UPI Radio Network, before being named its Midwest Bureau Chief in Chicago. He has covered numerous national and international events and his reports can be heard on affiliated stations throughout the world.

James Taylor—the one man dog—in 1971.

Island Boomers—
They Came, They Saw,
They Acculturated

BY GERALD R. KELLY

The Age of Aquarius dawned on the Island in 1967 with the coming of the Hairs, a pair of strong young men unlike anything the Vineyard had seen before: long, flowing locks, unshakeable macho images, quiet-spoken, polite and oblivious to the American Dream. They had tuned in, turned on and dropped out.

The Hairs got summer jobs working for Everett Whiting, the sage and a selectman of West Tisbury. To Whiting's astonishment, the Hairs thrived on hard work in the open air. They slaved at their jobs and were blissfully happy.

The Hairs were Tim Gibbons and Dick Benton of Vermont. They had records of all the best, newest music of the era. They spent an ice-cold winter in the old Navy bunker atop Peaked Hill, warmed by a wood stove and rendered content by marijuana which then had to be imported.

"They were idolized by the young people," Peter Huntington of Chilmark recalls. John Scannell of West Tisbury invited them here and introduced them around. His sister Julie later married Tim.

The Hairs were also esteemed by adults who placed great store in the Work Ethic, for the Hairs were the hardest working farmers around and in great demand at almost every up-Island farm. Never mind the shoulder-length locks or the occasional glazed-over eyes. They worked. They were happy.

Not a long time later, the Baby Boomers were here in full force. The Boom began after World War II, when hundreds of thousands of young men came back from Europe, then from the Pacific—world conquerors. For four long years, plans had been postponed. Marriages were hasty and babies were often accidental. It would all have to wait for the end of WWII.

In the summer of 1945, hostilities ceased and a nationwide lovefest began as young America reunited, coupled, and wed.

"Be fruitful and multiply, and replenish the earth, and subdue it," said the first chapter of the Good Book. These young people had already subdued the earth and now were out to replenish it. It was their third great victory, right after VE Day and VJ Day.

It was the beginning of the Baby Boom, which has been described inelegantly as the pig in the python, a great, huge bulge in the population of America which inched along from decade to decade, changing the nature of the brute as it went.

By 1965, the Boomers were 20 or so and rebellious, as people of that age have been throughout history. But this time, they were the all powerful pig in the python, able to have their own way and do their own thing. In the 60's and 70's, youth took over the country, shaped its arts, changed its consciousness and forged its conscience.

They had a sexual revolution, stopped a bloody war, drove the bouffant hair styles out of business and did drugs blithely and in full view of the world. "We shall overcome," they chanted and the peace cry still echoes off the Berlin Wall, cracking the iron curtain like the Liberty Bell.

Martha's Vineyard was a paradise for

the Baby Boomers of the early 70's. They flooded the Vineyard in the summer and found a curiously peaceful, idyllic place where they could dig for clams, dive for lobster, fish for bass, pitch tents in the woods and commune with nature.

No one bothered them. The occasional drug raids were as mild as the drug offenses. Kids blissed out on the beaches and became one with nature, stark naked at Jungle Beach where the natives cared not a whit.

The Vineyard had a long history of nude bathing. Jungle Beach was named after the long trails from South Road down to South Beach, through jungle-like growth. The trails had been blazed by summer residents of Barn House, an intellectual commune founded by Roger Baldwin, who also founded the Civil Liberties Union. Anyone from Barn House who sunbathed clad would have been viewed as a prude.

Up at Zack's Beach, Gay Headers had always been casually nude in the sun. Max Eastman, liberal sage, once had a visit from e. e. cummings, the English radical poet who was totally conventional in dress. They appeared on the Beach together, Max wearing skin and an intellectual air and e. e. cummings completely clad in suit, vest, tie and spats. Each was marvelously indifferent to the other's attire.

Youngsters who flocked here in the 70's were accustomed to shocking their elders but here, when they joined the Sexual Revolution, nobody seemed to notice and certainly nobody cared.

In 1969, a big old wooden building on Beach Road was taken over by Baby Boomers. Peter Simon started Martha's

*Afternoon frolic in
Gay Head.*

Midsummer Film Festival there and showed art and left-wing movies for two summers. The idea was to have fun and break even, not make money. They had impromptu free dances, including one at which the music of the Grateful Dead was played. About 150 youngsters crowded in to listen. Carly Simon and Livingston Taylor performed there together in informal fashion long before either became well known off-Island. That summer Peter and a few friends from college rented the old rambling Vanderhoop homestead in Gay Head. Soon there was a happy retinue of about 12 people who lived together, sunbathed together, danced, laughed, sang, philosophized, tripped, fished, swam, made love and had clam bakes and communal feasts together every night.

Most of them were wonderfully chaotic. Great beach fires were built and stones heated and wet seaweed was heaped on the rocks to steam and a canvas was dragged over it all to keep in the clambake heat and it was all left for about six hours before someone discovered that with all the tasks assigned, no one had been instructed to add the clams and lobsters. No matter. Clams were still good raw.

"The hippy ethic at the time was to enjoy life to the utmost, while making a living was a lesser priority," said Peter. "Back then, when rentals were within reason, we had the summer of a lifetime, and somehow managed to make ends meet with the movie theater. Quite an achievement considering our altered states of mind."

That same year James Taylor gave a free concert at the Tradewind Airport in Oak Bluffs. He was the Poet Laureate and voice of the Baby Boomers and he was Island. When he built a house in the woods in Tisbury, only friends or friends of friends—or friends of friends of friends—knew that the hand-painted sign of a hand with a pointed finger with the word "PUSH" led to his hideaway at the end of a long, winding road. Everyone in the No Jets construction crew that built the house was named in a song James made famous. Only Islanders knew that "Sweet Baby James," was his brother Alex's baby, not himself. And they were quite smug and comfortable about their inside track to James.

In West Tisbury, local kids demonstrated social conscience with well-aimed outrage at littering, a prelude to Earth Day. At that time, summer visitors were accustomed to throwing bottles out car windows and sides of roads were trash lanes. Three youngsters gathered up huge plastic bags of litter from the sides of the road and dragged it into Edgartown where they carefully laid it out on the steps of the courthouse in a well-mannered protest.

They were arrested for littering.

A few days later, an understanding judge let them off for good intentions. They had already been released from the county jail on their own recognizance. They were indignant, but too Islandized to organize.

Mal Jones, in West Tisbury, thought the hippy generation, as they were called back then, should have a free home here. On a large tract of his land, he bulldozed a huge loop of a road he called the doughnut. People could pitch their tents in the interior of the doughnut and live free, if not easy.

He devised an outhouse rigged to a chain which was hooked to a jack and a crank. A person using the outhouse, used a small shovel to cover the traces with dirt, then gave the crank a few jerks and the entire outhouse moved slowly— ecologically—through the woods, leaving a fertilized trail behind it, but no pollution.

Free was the key. At the West Tisbury Fair, some Boomers set up a booth and gave away food which was happily accepted by fellow Boomers but viewed askance by the older generation who firmly believed there is no free lunch.

Except at the Holy Ghost Society's annual festival where *sopa* was given away to all comers on Sunday. At the height of the summer flood of Baby Boomers, they were swamped with flower children lining up for freebies, but if the Portuguese-American hosts were nonplused by the long hair and outlandish costumes of

Mal Jones in 1980.

Thaw Malin, one of the Island's more popular artists, sets up shop at the Cliffs.

Robbie MacGregor providing trancelike tunes for the Renaissance Fair at the Art Worker's Guild in 1974.

their surprise guests, they fed everyone who came.

James Taylor financed the building of a huge garage he called Nobnocket on State Road in Tisbury. It was started as a foreign car repair shop, but later fell into disuse. One year, James Taylor held an informal community concert there, with people sitting on the edge of the car pit or on the dirt floor of the building.

Later, the garage became the Artworkers Guild, and was honeycombed with studios, galleries and darkrooms. A small restaurant, Helios, opened at the front and served Greek food and copious quantities of good will.

Thaw Malin, now a prospering artist, heard about the guild when he was still doing graduate work at the University of Georgia. He came here in 1974, visited the guild and moved in just in time to help lay the beams and nail plywood floors and sides to create the upstairs gallery booths. When he finished his labors, a corner gallery became available and he moved into that and started his labors again.

There were about 14 artists at a time at the guild and the outside walls sometimes had an eccentric appearance because each new artist remodeled his "space" to suit his needs and tempera-

ment and sometimes this meant new parameters.

Banker William Honey of the Martha's Vineyard National Bank was the guiding business light of the venture. He went there regularly to make sure that the non-businesslike artists were able to put their acts together in a reasonable way that would allow it all to fly. Other town officials helped by not taking explicit notice of what was going on there, overlooking the precise letter of the law. Malin recalls the benign neglect of Craig Kingsbury and Freeman Leonard, in particular.

Among the artists who belonged to the the bustling, creative project: Travis Tuck, Peter Eldridge, Fred Carelli, Robbie MacGregor, Anna Edey, Laurie Miller, Julie Mitchell, George Moffett, Charlie Finnerty, Arlene Sibley, Ruffy Eakins, Sanford Evans, Claire Thatcher, Ronni Simon and Andrea Wright.

Mia Farrow's brother Jonathan attended many guild meetings and painted glowing pictures of the California events called Renaissance Fairs, which he wanted the guild to sponsor. His accounts were so glowing and his enthusiasm so contagious, the idea gained momentum and the fair gradually took shape. In 1974, the Renaissance Fair was held, a marvelous Baby Boomer haute happening. The land around the Artworkers Guild was laced with trails and paths around which visitors strolled, being entertained—free, for the most part—by jugglers, acrobats, stilt-walkers, mimes, clowns, singers, lutists, flautists and the ubiquitous, all American guitar.

Sometime in the late 70's, the Baby Boomers lost their youthful glow. The pig in the python was entering maturity, sometimes kicking and screaming, but the process was inevitable. Because the Vineyard's cultural revolution had been peaceable and quiet in this "hip" pocket, the end of it was uneventful. People moved, got jobs, started businesses, had kids and just plain got older.

The Hairs moved to California and got rich in an exterminator business. Peter Huntington said they both rode around in Cadillacs and learned how to handle success.

Thaw Malin stayed on and built a solar house down the road from the old "PUSH" sign. Then he added a large studio to continue creating his distinctive flower paintings.

Anna Edey came here in 1972 and was one of the founders of the Artworkers Guild. A near tragedy in 1979 was the burning of her West Tisbury house, but this was transformed into a major asset. She rebuilt it in 1980 according to new, experimental principals she had developed and new concepts of waste management, heating and growing food. It was so successful she built a greenhouse in 1983 and expanded the concepts into a thriving business, Solviva, which means "sunlife." "I have proven my point, that you can grow food here in the middle of the winter without polluting anything and make a living at it," says Anna.

Elise LeBovit arrived on the Island with Richard Skidmore in 1974 from Virginia to make a demo record of the song, "Walking On Sunset," which became a local hit. She developed her talent as a masseuse as well as assisted Dr. Nancy Berger in her alternative healing practice. In 1986 Elise bought a large piece of land overlooking Gay Head beach and transformed an old farmhouse into a small health-oriented bed and breakfast/new age spa. The Duck Inn's decor is Cape Cod, Southwest, Japanese, Gay Head and duck. "I designed the Inn for Vineyarders as well as off-Island guests," describes Elise. "They can retreat to the wild wonders of Gay Head, where wildlife, the ocean, the cliffs and the lighthouse meet to express the peaceful and natural side of the Island." She has recently become involved in the "Save the cliffs" movement, which are now in danger of being developed.

Mitch Posin and John Abrams came here from a hippie commune in Vermont and started the South Mountain Company. After a while, Mitch Posin left South Mountain to start the Allen Farm Sheep & Wool Company with his wife, Clarissa Allen. One immediate benefit for all was the clearing of the Chilmark fields from South Road down to a clear,

Anna Edey carefully nurtures her young seedlings at "Solviva" during the middle of winter.

Elise LeBovit, proprietor of the "Duck Inn" in Gay Head, an alternative retreat geared for the "new age" population.

Mitch Posin and Clarissa Allen (a native Islander) who used their "back to the basics" philosophy to found the popular Allen Farm Sheep & Wool Company in Chilmark.

unimpeded, quite glorious view of all the Atlantic from the road. An Island rarity. John Abrams' South Mountain Company is now building affordable housing of a practical nature.

Peter Simon finally settled down, married, and is a productive photographer, author, publisher and father.

Robby MacGregor, who played lute at the Renaissance Fair, became a successful Vineyard contractor.

Carol Dodd Brush, who managed a cheese shop at Martha's Midsummer Film Festival, went on to open a cheese shop called Martha's Cheeses in Vineyard Haven, then a restaurant in Edgartown which was called Martha's Cheeses and Restaurant. She sold what is now known as Martha's Restaurant to raise her three children.

The Black Dog, built of massive beams on the harbor, was a rallying place for young Boomers as they came here, washing dishes and waiting on tables. In the early 70's, Vineyard amateur cooks took turns hosting special nights at the Black Dog with Mexican, Chinese, Greek and Indian foods. It still thrives, though Alan Miller, who built it, now has a cafe in Key West, Florida.

The sexual revolution was killed by AIDS. The drug culture was killed by crack pushers and violence. The rock and roll generation who thrived at Woodstock was replaced by heavy metal, and mindless post disco fare. But radio station WMVY still caters to the Baby Boomers who live on the Vineyard year-round. Their "album music" format concentrates on music of the late 60's and 70's—the Beatles, Rolling Stones, Grateful Dead, Neil Young, Bob Dylan, Van Morrison and James Taylor. On the Cape, radio stations cater to the later fans of Bon Jovi, Aerosmith and Madonna or those who came before the Boomers—Frank Sinatra, Elvis Presley and Buddy Holly. Here WMVY still sings the siren songs of the Seventies to the Boomers among us.

The Baby Boomers shaped Vineyard thinking, with people who moved here in the early 70's concentrating on whole aspects of the environmental movement, including recycling, alternative energy, water quality protection, coastal protection and small farming. They mostly fit nicely into the Island's self-image as a gentle oasis in a harsh world. With them came their art and music and their love of natural born beauty. Some prospered; some tread water. Some married; some split. There was, after all, to every thing a season—a time to be born, a time to plant, and a time to pick up that which is planted.

WMVY personalities Ken Goldberg (top), Tom Sheridan and Sarah Owens revel in the sounds of the late 60's. Even current music heard over the airwaves is carefully selected to appeal specifically to the aging boomer demographic.

Gerald R. Kelly is the co-author of Miss Elizabeth *and* File on Spratling, *both published by Little, Brown and Company. After moving to the Vineyard, a giant step ahead of the Boomers, he started the weekly newspaper,* The Grapevine, *on Earth Day, 1970. He is currently the lifestyle editor of* The Martha's Vineyard Times.

Even though the "alternative culture" is fast becoming middle aged, the quality of sharing that sparked many souls still lingers.

Some natives give tourists the "cold shoulder."

"Year-Rounder Solves Island Problems!"
(film at eleven)

BY VICTOR PISANO

Two years ago, I decided to become a year-rounder. It was an easy decision to make, precipitated as it was by a need to be near a very lovely lady who had just become a year-rounder herself. Otherwise, I would have remained as I had always been—a member of a rare breed of folk around these parts called Contrary Vineyarders. Contrary Vineyarders get their name from the Contrary Warriors of the Great Plains, a brotherhood of Native Americans who did *everything* backwards including riding into battle. Like them, I would back my Mustang onto the *Katama* freight boat in Wood's Hole every September and then back if off again every June, leaving the Island to the people who drove on straight every summer. The "on" season for me was "off" season, reserved for myself and a few other oblique diehards only heard about in local folklore. As a writer, the off season held a special attraction for me—the solitude, the inspiration, the anonymity, not to mention the romantic allure of it all. It was that particular temptation which finally turned my car around and kept it here for good.

Consensus has it that the Island goes from 10,000 people in the off season to 80,000 people during the summer months. I've heard other numbers, some higher, some lower. But, the fact that this tiny glacial dump swells eight to tenfold every school vacation never ceases to amaze me. I have tried gallantly not to automatically assume the year-rounders glazed expression each time June first rolls around. It's not easy. Just when the urge to throw back the shutters and fill your lungs with sunlight hits you, you're greeted instead with that horrific thought: "Thceerree baaaaaack."

Don't get me wrong. Some nice folks return here each year and some wonderfully creative talent as well, each hoping to capture that which is so readily available in the off season. But it's not the same. What they end up experiencing are a lot of leftover problems which get recycled back on to the Island with each summer ferry that arrives. With all due respect to the "personalities," "celebs," and other seasonals who arrive every thaw, year-rounders nevertheless still come to view summer residents as vaguely familiar faces who show up for dinner and then suddenly disappear when it comes time to clear the table.

Every year-rounder knows that the off season *officially* comes to an end as soon as the local tabloids headline pending disasters due to the expected overtaxing of the Island and its support systems by the hoards. "MOPED BAN HITS SKIDS," "LONGEST LINE IN STANDBY HISTORY," "FIVE CORNER GRIDLOCK RIVALS TIME SQUARE," "BOMBS UNCOVERED BY SOUTH BEACH BATHERS!" What are the rest of us supposed to make of all this when the big off season headline reads, "WAMPANOAGS NIX CELLULAR PHONES." I mean think about it. The problems always seem overwhelmingly insurmountable and costly when compared to those that face us during the off season. No wonder we year-rounders cringe whenever we're asked, "So, what do you do

Daytrippers line up at Pier 44 for their return to New Bedford.

Idiot's delight.

around here in the off season?'' For this reason, having thought about it a great deal, I offer these simple, cost effective steps to solve *all* the Island problems in one fell swoop with no cost to the year-round resident taxpayer.

SOLUTIONS

1) Overcrowding: Simple, ban *The New York Times*! Anyone who can't go two weeks (or more) without all the news fit to print, shouldn't be in a place where hardly any of the news is fit to print and where the natives prefer it that way. Sure,

there would be some agonizing sounds in the streets—some death throes perhaps on Lucy Vincent Beach, but those worthy of their salt would survive for the betterment of all. They would come to their senses sooner or later and fully appreciate the reasons why they were trying to escape all that news in the first place. And those that couldn't handle a *Times*-ectomy cold turkey (which is most of them) would be happier knowing that there were a few hearty souls somewhere who could. Those that survive the operation would be eternally grateful. Besides, wouldn't it be a breath of fresh air to be able to walk down the aisle at Alley's General Store some Sunday in July without the fear of being crushed to death under collapsing walls of book review sections? There are other benefits as well—a real domino effect.

The *Islander* and all her sister ships would ride higher in the water and would have more room for additional cars (say 1,500 or more per season). The airport would see fewer jet flights. Our landfill and dump site problems would ease dramatically. Our waters and estuaries would thereby become cleaner. The clams would then be able to breath a lot easier. It boggles the mind how one simple rational act, with no cost to Island taxpayers, could have such widespread ramifications. Let's face it. Virtually all of our problems stem from this one dilemma. No one likes overcrowding and no one has any idea of how to curb it, until now. Ban the *Times*, I say.

2) Moped Rentals: In some local circles, the summer season is also referred to as "M and M" season, (Maps and Mopeds). They're on every corner, usually stopped and holding up traffic—daytrippers, wrestling with unruly four by five foot maps. And why is it that most of them look like they're trying to force confessions out of their mopeds instead of riding them? The brand name should be "Uncle!" They can't go far and they can't go fast—a lot of them simply can't go at all. But the biggest drawback is their sudden stops. I know of one volunteer paramedic who annually threatens to quit because rescuing moped victims has become a full time job in the summer. The perfect solution here is again simple and cheap—outlaw maps of the Island! Without maps, those who rent mopeds would be forced to circle the rental shops for hours or at least keep them in their line of sight. They would soon get bored going in circles and give up the idea. Also, outlawing maps would free up all the other island roads where mopeds frequently travel and where some end up as part of the landscape. If mopeders insist on maps, then I suggest creating a black market map and selling them only to moped renters at a premium price. These maps in reality would be bogus. They would show that there really are no other roads on the island other than those that circle the moped shop. They wouldn't feel bad for long though, because all the T-shirt and fudge shops within the vicinity would be accurately marked, thereby completing the ruse. There goes both the moped problem and the overtime duty for that poor paramedic. All this without hurting those merchants who consider the humming of mopeds music to their ears.

3) Traffic Flow: With *The New York Times* gone and no maps to indicate where, most of the current traffic flow problems would automatically disappear. However, if there were any residual snags, there is yet another painfully simple solution. The idea was already tried in a manner without anyone being aware of it. It was implemented by the powers that be in Edgartown when they created a local uproar by changing the one way street signs to the ire of some townspeople and a lot of others. They had the right idea, only they didn't follow through properly. It was completed more successfully back in the mid-seventies—a truly amazing thing to watch. I was doing my graduate work in Rome, where daily headlines proclaimed imminent doom. What Rome had managed to preserve for more than two thousand years was crumbling all around them in a matter of only a few. Car pollution was literally eating away the Eternal City. Like the Island on a

Traffic jams of epic proportion on the outskirts of downtown Vineyard Haven.

grander scale, the problem was to curtail traffic flow—better yet, eliminate it from the central city all together. What they did took genius and courage—change all the one way street signs at random, every few days. The confusion and gridlock it created was monumental. Roman drivers became so frustrated and angry, hundreds actually walked away from their cars right on the spot! For months, some say years, Rome's traffic eased. No one in their right minds would go in with a car. Why they stopped the policy in the eighties is a mystery to me. Can you imagine what this island would be like the first few days with random changes in one way street signs? Complete pandemonium. Pretty soon—"Hey, Honey. Let's leave our car in Wood's Hole this time." What's the cost of flipping a few signs once in a while?

There probably won't be film at eleven —too bad, really. But in the long run, the Island will reflect those who choose to stay behind every winter to clean the table. They're a resilient group who don't take kindly to congestion, hit and run merchants, or boats named, "*Spray*."

Victor Pisano, born and raised in New England, has an extensive background in television production and screenwriting. Some of his noted credits are James Taylor in Concert *(PBS) and the mini-series* Three Sovereigns For Sarah. *He is currently writing a cookbook and a screenplay and lives with his wife, Judy Belushi, in Vineyard Haven.*

Housebroken

BY PETER FEIBLEMAN

About three years after I'd moved out of a city apartment into a house on the Vineyard, I decided it would be nice to have a guest cottage on my property—far enough from the main house to afford me some privacy, close enough to make visitors feel at home. I didn't want anything large or expensive, just a modest affair with a bedroom or two—and while I was at it, perhaps a tiny living room and

Peter Feibleman's guest house arises, against all odds.

kitchen in case the guests wanted to cook or be by themselves—and maybe one small room with a separate entrance that could serve as a study for me.

"In other words, another main house," the architect said.

"Definitely not," I said. "Nothing like that. A *guest* house—that's all I want. You're thinking too big. Think small."

"How small are your guests?"

"Let's not be silly," I said.

"Okay," the architect said, "you want two bedrooms, a living room, a kitchen, and a study. How many bathrooms do you want?"

"I haven't thought about it."

"Think about it," the architect said.

"Okay," I said. "Two bathrooms."

"All in all, that'll mean three stories," the architect said, looking at a surveyor's map. "Your zoning board won't allow a guest house that's larger in territorial circumference than one half your original house."

"What's a zoning board?" I said.

The architect stared at me. "How old are you?" he said.

"What's that got to do with it?"

"Nothing, I guess," he said. "Trust me. Don't try to understand it. The living room and kitchen can be on the first floor, the two bedrooms on the second, your study on the third. Where do you want your two bathrooms?"

"I haven't thought about it."

"Think about it," the architect said.

"Okay," I said. "One bathroom between the two bedrooms, another one in the study."

"How about the main floor? Do you want people to walk upstairs whenever they have to go, or do you want a half bath down there?"

"What's a half bath?" I said.

The architect stared at me.

"What I mean is," I said, "what's the difference between a half bath and a toilet?"

"Look," he said after a moment, "maybe I'd better just go home and rough out a design for what I think you want. We'll take it from there."

That sounded fine, and a couple of weeks later the architect appeared with some rolled-up drawings under his arm. He spread out the first drawing on my dining room table, and I sat down and examined it in silence for several minutes.

"It doesn't look tall for three stories," I said, "does it?"

The architect swallowed. "That's not a cross section," he said. "That's a floor plan. Please don't tell me you don't know what a floor plan is. Please don't."

"There's no use getting that hysterical sound in your voice every time I say something," I said. "We'll never get anything done."

"I'm sorry," the architect said. "I'll try to pull myself together."

"The truth is I've never built a house before, so I've never sat down with anybody like you."

"I've never sat down with anybody like you either," the architect said.

A few weeks later—after a period of chaos made up of two parts misunderstanding and one part bewilderment—the architect and I reached an agreement, and everything was ready to go. "So I guess in a month it'll be built," I said, "right?"

"Well, I wouldn't exactly say *built*," the architect said. "More like *begun*. First we need the permits. You'd better talk to your neighbors—so they won't object to your guest house when they're notified by the zoning committee."

"Why would they object?"

"Just talk to them," he said. "Nicely," he added. "You don't want to give them the idea that you'll have a lot of noisy construction going on."

"Will I have a lot of noisy construction going on?"

"Yes," the architect said.

My friend Phyllis is more diplomatic and delicate with people than I am, so I asked her to come for the weekend while I invited all my neighbors to dinner, one by one, telling each about the new house, minimizing its importance, and emphasizing its daintiness and minute size. "The truth is, Peter shouldn't call it a guest house," Phyllis told one couple with her most winning smile. "It's just a kind of doll's house. Barely a cottage."

"No, it isn't," I said.

"Yes, it is," Phyllis said, stuffing a sandwich in my mouth. "Peter has no sense of proportion."

After the neighbors were taken care of, Phyllis went home, and the architect prepared to present his proposal to the town zoning board. The members of the board had other jobs during the day, so they only met at night; the contractor and I went along with the architect, and we sat in a small dark room on wooden chairs facing them. Nobody spoke above a whisper until the meeting was called to order and then things went smoothly until the members of the board asked if there were any objections to the proposal. A woman from the neighborhood stood up and said that her husband wanted her to make sure I wasn't going to use the guest house for commercial purposes, and I said I wasn't and please to tell her husband. The members of the board listened in a profound, expressionless way, like a jury on television, and took a vote; they said they'd mail me their official decision within 14 days.

"That's a yes," the architect said on the way out. "Looks like you've got your building permit."

"What about the board of health?" the contractor said.

"Should be automatic," the architect told him. "As I see it, we'll be ready to break ground in ten days."

That night I got a phone call from my old friend Ira in Los Angeles. For three years Ira had been building a house in the hills, held up every few weeks by an apparently unending series of disasters, most of them spurred on by, and tangled up in, bureaucratic red tape. "Watch out for the board of health," he said when I told him my news. "It's little people in big jobs. Civil servants are all underpaid —you'll be like the smell of blood to a shark that's been living on garbage."

"Steady," I said.

"Don't tell me 'steady,'" Ira said, his voice rising. "I've driven downtown to see one board or another 43 times in three years, and I *still* don't have my permits."

"Things are different here," I said in a calming tone. "This isn't a big city, it's a quiet little island in winter, and country people are nice. My neighbors treat me like Caesar."

"Beware the Ides of March," Ira said.

A year later I began to wonder whether he had cast a particularly disgusting spell on me. By then the board of health had attacked my project with a vengeance so petty it could only be the product of some dark design. First they claimed my property was too small for two septic systems. (We got a lawyer and proved them wrong.) Second, my original septic tank was too close to the harbor. (They got a surveyor and proved themselves wrong.) Third, a small part of my property was beach, causing the whole thing to be classified as wetlands, with a maximum of three bedrooms allowed on it, including those in the main house. (We had to get a coastal survey, a geological survey, *and* a lawyer to disprove that one.) Fourth, they okayed my guest house on condition that I move my original septic system 60 feet up the hill I live on and 40 feet back. By that time I'd spent a small fortune on surveyors and engineers (forget my lawyer), and complying with the new demand would have cost $30,000 more, never mind listening to the sound of raw sewage being pumped up around me for the rest of my life. (The lawyer threatened to sue the board for harassment, and they dropped it.)

Fifth, they issued me a building permit—then rescinded it the day after we'd broken ground.

"Can they do that?" I asked.

"No," the lawyer said. "But they've done it—this time we *will* sue them."

"A lawsuit won't help me," I said. "I'd spend the rest of my guest-house budget on legal fees."

"I won't be charging you," he said. "This is a matter of principle for me."

"The board of health doesn't have any principles," the contractor said. "They're cashing in on the ecology market." He was standing with us, looking down at the huge gaping wound he'd opened in what had once been my backyard—a hole 28 feet long, 18 feet wide, and 6 feet deep. "It's a good thing I got that dug before the snow starts," he added. "If I'd waited another week, the ground would be frozen and we'd have to put this off till spring. Who at the board of health hates you?"

"I don't know," I said.

"Let's find out," the lawyer said. "It might be helpful."

We all trooped down to the next meeting of the board of health and sat facing a table of sullen people with angry eyes, jutting chins, and folded arms. The committee was composed of a woman named (let us say) Mrs. Snear, who looked (I thought) not unlike Margaret Hamilton in *The Wizard of Oz*, and several men who looked like her monkeys. Our attendance was a waste of time, but on the way home I stopped to have a few drinks with a friend, got a little tight, laughed and joked about all my troubles with the board of health, walked home feeling much better, and fell into the hole in my backyard.

"It's not very serious. The swelling will go down in a month or so," the doctor said, peering at the X rays of my knee. "Your shoulder may take a little longer— stay prone for a while and see how it goes."

Eight weeks later I was in bed with four pill bottles, a pile of books, a pizza, a cheeseburger with French fries, and a chocolate malt, when the lawyer phoned. "Good news," he said.

"Are all the members of the board of health alive?"

"Yes."

"Then it's not good news," I said.

"It's like this," the lawyer said. "I phoned Mrs. Snear and asked what was at the bottom of the whole thing. She said the original owner wrote the board some nasty letters ten years ago about the smell of rotting seaweed on the beach."

It's hard to appreciate some of the Island's finer things when constantly being distracted by construction concerns.

"That's *all*?"

"No," he said. "You complained to them yourself once—when your garbage wasn't picked up for a month."

"So *that's* it."

"No," he said. "They could have overlooked all that. Mrs. Snear said you only made one unforgivable mistake—you hired me. It's *me* they're angry at, not you. They claim I put an illegal cesspool on *my* beach property."

"Did you?"

"No," he said. "I don't own beach property—they had me mixed up with some other guy who has the same last name."

A couple of days after that, the building permit was issued again, and work began on my guest house. After waiting so long the builders were anxious to show their enthusiasm. They worked feverishly all week, and I was touched to see so many loyal people on my side. On Monday they accidentally cut through the TV cable, on Tuesday they knocked out my phone system, and by Saturday I had no electricity. That night the foreman and one of the workers came down to express their sincere regret. "Never mind," I said, gulping some aspirin, "you didn't do it on purpose—I'll manage as long as I have water."

"You have plenty of water," the foreman said cheerfully, pointing to a lake forming up the hill behind him.

"You just don't have any in your pipes," the worker said. "Not since we cut through the main. Do you happen to have any sandbags in the house?"

Peter Feibleman is a novelist who grew up in New Orleans, spent many years in Spain, New York and Los Angeles before settling on the Island. His most recent book, Lilly *(William Morrow), details his fascinating relationship with the legendary Lillian Hellman.*

Aboard the ferry to Chappy.

168

Edgartown:
Leather and Lace

BY PHILIP R. CRAIG

In 1955 I saw Edgartown for the first time. I had followed a beautiful girl down to Martha's Vineyard from Boston that spring after college let out. I had never been on an island before and expected this one to be a barren place with perhaps one palm tree growing in the middle. I was surprised by the truth. Similarly, I was surprised by Edgartown. Having just come from Boston and before that from the arid mesa country of southwestern Colorado, I was astonished to find myself in a town where everything was clean and neat. No dust in the air. No garbage in the streets, no weeds growing in the yards, no disintegrating buildings with broken windows; the streets were narrow and neat, the houses well maintained, the lawns green and the flower boxes and gardens already bright with blooms. I'd never seen any place like it. I got a job with George T. Silva, working on his scow, and spent the best part of that summer repairing docks wrecked by the 1954 hurricanes. I've been in Edgartown every summer but one since then. The summer I missed was in 1957 when I took the beautiful girl out to Colorado to meet my family. That winter I married her and the next summer we were back on the Island. She and her father and grandfather were born on the Island and our children were born there. I am the only off-Islander in the family, but you must blame my parents for that, not me.

The Edgartown pictured on postcards reminds me of a little old lady wearing lace. There's something prim and proper about the town. Its dress is buttoned to the neck. Its shoes are the high, laced kind. Its skirts are long. It has a sense of propriety, of its place in society, and a knowledge of money and family stature. It disapproves of loud bars, loud parties

and all such vulgarities, believing such activities more properly belong in Oak Bluffs. Edgartown prefers cocktail parties attended by ladies in pastel clothing and gentlemen in bright slacks and blazers. It is, as William Styron perceived, a bit stuffy.

It's also so crowded with tourists that in the summer my wife and I only go down town when there is absolutely no way to avoid it. For example, when we want to go sailing. Then we have to sneak down Cooke Street to Collins Beach, where we keep our dinghy, park the Jeep and row out to our little red cutter, the *Gate of Horn*, which swings on her stake between the Yacht Club and the Reading Room. Then we sail off down harbor, or outside over to Cape Pogue Pond for an over-night. When our cruise is over, we scurry back out of town along Cooke Street.

We like the town best in the fall when its famous captains houses are silent and closed, its harbor largely empty of the yachts that fill it from June through September and many of its shops shut. It's emptied of tourists and has been returned to the people we know, its year-round inhabitants who actually make it work, who keep the peace, fight the fires, maintain the great houses, clean the streets and fight the paper wars in the town hall. Scallop boats have replaced the yachts and fishermen occupy the parking lot at the foot of Main Street where the bass and bluefish derby has its weigh-in station.

Groups of local men still gather in the mornings. One group meets at Midway Market where they can gas up their cars and get fresh coffee and newspapers. Golfers and policemen seem to favor that spot. Down on Main Street, across from the town hall, another group, this one few

A grove of apple blossoms surrounds the Old Whaling Church (top).

The Captain Fisher House on North Water Street.

down, giving us a moment of high excitement as we wondered if all of Al's booze would soon be going up in smoke. Since those days, downtown Edgartown has changed a lot. Its once small-town Main Street has given up the stores that served the needs of its year-round residents and has replaced them with shops which cater to well-heeled summer tourists. Except for the hardware store, most of the stores you *need* are now out at the edge of town.

When I first worked at Al's, the post office, two drug stores, two grocery stores and three (!) liquor stores were on lower Main Street. Now one drug store has been replaced by a T-shirt shop and the other no longer sells drugs but only sundries. The A & P has long since moved to upper Main Street and Connors' Market, which later became the Edgartown Market, is a shadow of its former self and is buried behind some Main Street tourist shops. Al's Package Store, no longer tiny, is now located opposite the A & P and left-turning customers are the cause of a continual traffic jam. The Harborside Liquor Store, formerly at the four corners downtown and once the first and most important shopping stop for newly arrived yachtsmen, is now a commuting distance to town, at the triangle near the new post office and the town's only pharmacy.

The stores downtown these days are expensive boutiques and shops selling imported sweaters, yachting clothes, exotic gadgets and souvenirs. And even these shops change each year as rents go higher and the shop owners are obliged to fold their tents and give way to more affluent renters seeking their share of the tourist dollars that come pouring into town each summer.

For a town so dependent upon summer tourists, Edgartown is consciously uncooperative with them. It is a reflection of its character that it shunts day tripping and sightseeing busses off onto side streets and is infamous for its lack of public toilet facilities. When I first visited the town in 1955, the issue of building public toilets downtown was being hotly debated. In 1990 the subject is still being debated and toilets have not been built.

in number and apparently needing no coffee, leans against a wall or lamppost in the comfortable configuration that speaks of old friendships. A third group sits in front of the Dock Street Coffee Shop and discusses town affairs, discoursing at length upon matters great and small in the manner of town fathers. When the weather gets colder, the men move indoors or to sunny spots where they can eat doughnuts and drink coffee out of the wind.

For many of my first summers in Edgartown I worked in Al's Package Store, which was then a tiny place on Main Street just a couple of doors away from the movie house which later burned

Similarly, the town is notorious for the costs of its harbor moorings and for its lack of facilities for visiting yachtsmen. When my wife and I sail our little cutter to Nantucket, we find free and well maintained toilets and cold water showers at the end of the pier leading to the dock where we tie our dinghy. Edgartown offers no such hospitality to its sailing visitors and has no plans to do so. Rather than appeal to such transients, Edgartown prefers to cater to the summer long visitors who own their own homes and whose yachts are on their own moorings. Oak Bluffs is the town for migrants; not Edgartown.

Still, Edgartown harbor is a magnet for wandering yachts, and its yacht club is host to racers and cruisers. Beautiful boats fill the harbor during racing and cruising weeks and during these times I have learned to lock up the dinghy we keep on Collins Beach down by the Reading Room (a gentlemen's club where, it has been said, the only reading materials are the labels of bottles). The lock is necessary to prevent visiting yachtsmen from stealing the dinghy late at night to return to their boats and then setting the dinghy adrift once they're out there. I lost a couple of pairs of oars and twice had my dinghy retrieved by local boatmen before

Edgartown harbor sports dazzling boats throughout the season.

I began my current practice of log-chaining my boat to the dock during racing and regatta weeks. So much for the honor and sportsmanship of the yachting set.

Yet the yachts are lovely and I like to take the *Gate of Horn* down through the harbor to look at the million dollar racing machines, the big power cruisers, the day sailors and, best of all, the blue water cruising sailboats. I admire Walter Cronkite's fine yacht and am pleased that he is actually a sailor, not just another rich guy who hires a crew of young towheads to run his boat for him. If I'm taking my

guests for a harbor cruise, we all stare aghast at the colossal house on the harbor being built by a New England business-man whose millions, unlike those of the more reserved owners of the Water Street mansions, are on display for all to see. Such ostentation in Edgartown is cause for both alarm and secret joy. How dare he? What will he do next? Is it true that he tries to rent out his private moorings to visiting boatmen? Scandal!

Islanders do not have much to do with sailboats. They are power boat people. They *use* their boats for fishing and, during the summer when they earn most of the money they spend in the winter, have no time for such leisurely pursuits as sailing. Although my wife and I also own a fine slightly beat-up 17-foot lapstrake outboard motorboat which we employ each year to capture shellfish in various Edgartown ponds, my sailboat is a sure sign that I am a summer gink and not a year-rounder.

The graceful tourist town which borders Edgartown harbor may wear lace, but there's a leathery side of the town too. Many Edgartownians, both the summer and year-round varieties, actually live off in the woods in new or old subdivisions. My wife and I, for example, summer in an old hunting camp in Ocean Heights, three miles from downtown Edgartown. We have a fine view of Sengekontacket

Remembrance of things past: a movie theatre on Main Street above the Town Hall.

Pond and tend to socialize with our immediate neighbors. Other citizens, including some Beans and Snopes never mentioned by the Chamber of Commerce, live on the great plains of Katama, or west of the Edgartown-Vineyard Haven road, or up by the water tower or off of Meeting House Way (Edgartown's worst car shattering corduroy road!) in places tourists never see. They live lives having little to do with the Vineyard advertised by the Chamber of Commerce. They garden, they work to support their families during the long winter when the tourist dollars are gone and live in houses buried in the woods or unnoticed beside the public roads.

People like Kenny Deitz and Kit and Mike Smith don't spend a lot of time hanging around downtown looking picturesque. They have work to do. Chauncey Maury, one of the only two geniuses I've ever known, lives amid an incredible accumulation of tools and whole and partial cars and machines out near the Herring Creek and never comes to town at all any more. Anyone with a mechanical problem or an electrical problem can take it to Chauncey and he can explain how to fix it. Half of the auto mechanics on the island take their troubles to Chauncey.

Some of the local folks live on Chappaquiddick, that sometimes island which jeep drivers reach by driving east along the beach from Katama and which everyone else can only get to by taking the Chappy ferry from Edgartown.

The Chappy ferry is both cute and functional. Tourists love it and we all use it at one time or another. There are really three or four Chappy ferries, the largest capable of taking up to four cars the hundred yards or so across the opening of Edgartown harbor to the Chappy landing. Each of these ferries is named the *On Time* and there are two rumors about why: The first is that the original ferry was completed on time and was so named in celebration and the second is that since the ferry has no schedule it's always on time. I like the second one best, so that's the one I give to off-Island visitors.

Chappy people make no bones about

preferring to be left alone. The worse curse that has ever come upon them was the accident involving Senator Kennedy twenty years ago at Dyke Bridge. Since then the Chappy people have had to put up with a steady stream of pilgrims seeking The True Bridge, where the faithful and hateful slice off slivers of the bridge for relics, hold memorial services on the anniversary of the accident, fill memento bottles of water from beneath the bridge and otherwise behave like half wits. The Chappy people wish the pilgrims would all go away and not return, because they like their privacy and want it back. Since the Dyke Bridge is falling apart so badly that soon it may not be there at all to attract visitors, so maybe the Chappy people's dream will come true. I wish them luck.

My wife and I go to Chappy to pick blueberries and beach plums and to fish. I won't tell you where we do our berry and plum picking, but we fish where the Edgartown regulars fish, on the long beaches of Chappaquiddick: Wasque Point, where the bluefish chase bait in the Wasque Rip; East Beach, where we fish Bernie's Point, the Jetties and Cape Pogue; Cape Pogue gut, the Cedars inside Cape Pogue Pond where, a few years back when there didn't seem to be fish anywhere else, we slaughtered three and four pound blues for days on end. (That was an odd year: the fish would be here for four

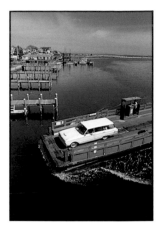

The "On Time" is, once again, on time.

The Dyke Bridge, a mere shell of its former self, is now closed to all forms of recreation.

Jim McCarthy, at work at Katama farm, restoring agriculture to the plains.

The Edgartown Lighthouse, symmetrically enclosed by the Chappaquiddick Beach Club.

der clams in Pocha Pond on Chappy. Together we dip net the best scallops in the world in Cape Pogue Pond, Katama Pond, Eel Pond and Sengekontacket, and at Thanksgiving I hook oysters in the Great Pond. The summer people catch themselves some steamers and quahogs, but we and the year-rounders really harvest the ponds.

And the same summer people envy the owners of the condominiums and houses that now line South Beach in Katama where not long ago there were only low dunes and flat, unbroken fields. They flock to South Beach, fly kites and wish that they owned those dwellings only a short walk from the sea. Those of us who remember the open spaces are only astonished at the clutter of buildings and wonder why anyone would want to build there. Thank God for Katama Farm, a working dairy farm whose very presence partially provides a balance of nature on the plains.

Yet, for all its changes and posturing, and though I try never to go downtown in the summertime, I still believe Edgartown is the Island's loveliest town. After thirty-five summers here I'm still a lot like a wide-eyed, first time tourist. I like the look of the great captain's houses on Water Street, the neat paint and shingles of its smaller houses, the clipped lawns and gardens of flowers. Even now, after all of these years, I'll sometimes stroll its narrow streets and brick sidewalks and admire its white churches, its white houses, its great pagoda tree or its waterfront. I'll walk out to lighthouse beach or past the offices of the *Vineyard Gazette*, where I'll wonder once again if that fine, insular newspaper would mention World War III if no Islander happened to become involved with it. I never tire of looking at boats in the Harbor and the Chappy ferry still fascinates me as does the town itself which, for all its self-conscious propriety, is a place of grace and beauty. Though most of the time I live a leathery Edgartown life in the woods or on the beach, I love to look at the lace.

or five days, then somewhere else for four or five days, then somewhere else yet again. Once you found them, they were there for days; then they were gone. We got a lot of them at the Cedars that year.)

And we shellfish, for Edgartown is blessed with the largest and richest shellfishing ponds on the Island and, I expect, of any New England town. While my wife suns and reads on the beach, I dig for steamers at the south end of Katama Pond and in Eel Pond and rake for littlenecks in Katama Pond and for stuffers and chow-

During the off-season Philip R. Craig and his wife live in Hamilton, Massachusetts while he teaches literature at Wheelock College in Boston. He has written for The Cape Cod Times *and has published two novels:* Gate of Ivory, Gate of Horn *and* A Beautiful Place to Die, *which is set on Martha's Vineyard. His second Martha's Vineyard novel,* The Woman Who Walked Into The Sea, *will soon be published by Charles Scribner's Sons.*

Floral arrangements adorn the Emily Post House on Fuller Street.

The Edgartown Lighthouse at dawn.

The Gay Head cliffs show their true colors.

Afternoon With Moshup

BY STEPHEN DAVIS

All this happened last September eighth. Late that day I was walking on a low-tide sandbar along the Atlantic beach of Gay Head. I'd been hiking for miles in the ankle-high water, from the tip of Squibnocket Point past Zack's Cliffs, The Sahara, the Max Eastman Memorial Nude Beach, Middle Beach, Behane Beach, Betty Beach, the 1135 Association Beach, Lillian Hellman Hut Beach and on up by the spot where Black Brook meanders into the sea. You know the place. Anyway, the sun was out and still high and everything was shining in four shades of blue. The water along the shore was azure, the sand-bar water was aqua, the deeper water was cobalt, like Venetian glass, and the sky was cerulean, streaked with cirrus.

Suddenly, over my left shoulder, I heard a roar. I looked up and saw a flight of five F-15 jets peel off formation and dive towards the isle of Nomans Land. Puffs of black smoke emitted from the jets like evil flatus, followed by concussion thumps as the practice bombs exploded just a few miles away. Blood clot! This was war.

Then there was an almost imperceptible blinding flash that coincided with what sounded like a sonic boom from one of the jets. Looking up, I was astonished to see a small tear-like fissure in the sheltering sky, from which tumbled a man-like object that landed in the sea with an awesome splash. When the object surfaced, about a half-mile from shore, it proceeded to swim toward the spot where I lingered. It came quickly, like a powerboat, but I could soon see it was a man, or something like a man, and it was swimming with such force that it left a considerable white-water wake. I rubbed my eyes, unsure whether I was having an out-of-body episode, but when I looked again this giant man was out of the froth and striding along the sandbar. He was *magnificent*, about eight feet tall, with a dark olive complexion and thick black eyebrows and hair, which he wore long and tied back. Exceedingly handsome, he also wore a sort of coronet composed of grasses, bird feathers, wampum and kelp. Before I could take any more in, he came up and said, "Kah-nae-que-tah! Nan-naw-weh-ak Akwinnah!"

Fortunately, during my school days, I had taken an honors degree in Algonquin languages at Dartmouth, so I knew what the giant was saying—"How're ya doin'? Great to be back in Gay Head!"—and found myself able to converse with this strange apparition.

"Wh-wh-who are you?" I asked tremulously.

"I am called Moshup," the being answered.

"Aren't you the god of this place?"

"I am He that Is," answered the giant, quoting the ancient formula.

"But I thought you left here hundreds of years ago," I said, somewhat unsteadily.

"That is true," Moshup said. "But that's only because I can't afford to live here. These days I rent out my place over by Witch Pond to some demi-gods from New York."

"So where do you now dwell?" I queried.

"Way across the Great Water, where the Cap of Spartel overlooks the Caves of Hercules in the land of the god Antaeus," Moshup replied.

Realizing this was an incredible opportunity, I decided to petition the god. "Tell me, Lord Moshup, what brings you here today?"

"Well, every few years or so, I like to

Part of the majestic Gay Head cliffs, from a different point of view.

178

come and visit my lands and my people, you know what I mean? I made this whole place you know, this Capawack land where we now stand. See those cliffs over there?" He pointed toward Gay Head, several hundred yards away. "See that red cliff there? That's where I used to kill and butcher the whales I used to catch back in the Old Times. That's how come it's all red." The god did a sort of quick double-take. "Say, where the heck is that red cliff anyway? It *used* to be there."

"It washed away some time ago," I said.

"Well, that's too bad. I'll kinda miss seeing that. But it's the way of the world: here today, gone tomorrow. Anyway, here it was that I settled, this here Akwinnah place, with my wife Skewanta and the kids—twelve sons, twelve daughters. For pets I had a white whale and a great big old toad that my enemy Chae-peh turned into that big rock over there, in the water where the cliffs start. But that's a long story. We grew corn and did some fishing and lived off the land and the sea. It was paradise! When the English came I said that's it, and we lit out."

"Why did you leave?" I asked.

"It was Christianity, pure and simple," the god said. "This Island wasn't big enough for me and Jesus, and that's all there was to it. Now, tell mc about my people."

"You mean the Gay Head Indians?" I asked.

"Yes, them. Tell me the news."

I had to be honest. "I don't know that much about it," I replied, "but recently they got back some of the land for the tribe."

"Got back from who?"

"From the town," I said. "For more than a hundred years some of the people's land belonged to the Town of Gay Head, and so the people went to court and had to prove they were a real tribe of Indians, and in the end they won a great victory and the land is theirs. But it was a difficult battle."

The god looked pensive, "Did many braves die in the battle?" he asked.

"No," I answered. "Nobody died."

"Good," he said. "Now, when do they

A juxtaposition of the Gay Head lighthouse and cliffs.

Donald and Patricia Malonson of the Aquinnah Wampanoag Tribal Council dressed in traditional ceremonial regalia.

get the rest of the Island?"

I told him I didn't know anything about that, and he said that he was happy his people were again at peace. Feeling mischievous, I explained to him, in terms he could comprehend, that there was still a problem with one small piece of land his people owned, which was surrounded by the lands of a very rich Dowager Queen who coveted their land for herself. "Where does she dwell?" he demanded, and I told him that her driveway gave onto Moshup's Trail.

"What's that?" he asked. "A road? They named it after me? Hey, that's great! I like that! But never mind, I shall go see this Dowager Queen and beg her to come to her senses." I wished him luck and started to split.

"Hey!" the god exclaimed. "Don't go. Tell me more."

I'm just a visitor here myself, I told him. Gay Head is a place where some very rich people live, and some people who aren't rich, and some people somewhere in the middle. I told him that Gay Head used to be rather remote—"In my day it was an Island!" the god interjected—but that now lots of people visited, especially in the summertime, and you could even get cable television.

"What's that?" Moshup asked, but I pretended not to hear him, because just then a big blue-and-white tour bus came

roaring by along Moshup's Trail on the way down from the Head. Then it was quiet again.

"Yep, looks like the old place has changed quite a bit," the god mused. He sat down on the sand and struck a contemplative pose. Just then, another flight

A sight to see.

180

of silver F-15's came streaking across the reddening sky, headed for another bombing run on Nomans. An annoyed expression briefly clouded the brow of the god, who absently pointed a finger at the lead jet, which began to lose altitude, sprouted a lone parachute, and exploded in a bright wheel of fire. "Damned insects," Moshup grumbled. "Always were terrible up here in the summer."

"Hey man," I said nervously, "I gotta motivate up the beach."

"Me too," the god said, getting to his feet and adjusting his loincloth. "Gotta visit the little wampum gal over in Lobsterville."

We shook hands and I bade the great god Moshup adieu. Last I saw him, he was leaping over a big dune that was bristling with *No Trespassing* signs. The next day, the following item appeared on page 10 of *The Boston Globe*:

Pilot Unhurt in Air Force Mystery

An Air Force Reserve F-15 from Burppleson AFB crashed into Vineyard Sound while on a routine training exercise, Reserve officials announced last night. The pilot, identified as Capt. Henry Sturkey, ejected safely over water and was rescued by the Menemsha-based Coast Guard vessel *Fraudulent*, which was on drug interception maneuvers just offshore. Captain Sturkey told reporters that it felt like his plane had been crushed "by the hand of God," and that he felt lucky to have survived.

Stephen Davis is an occasional Gay Head summer resident. He is the best-selling author of Hammer Of The Gods, *and other books. He is now at work on a novel set on Martha's Vineyard.*

Mark Widdis passes down traditional Wampanoag songs and stories to the next generation.

The West Tisbury Congregational Church.

A Stroll Through West Tisbury

BY EILEEN MALEY

The air is calm at this hour, it won't stir and then whistle down Music Street until about nine. At dawn, our wood stove's chimney smoke hangs straight up, the dog tugs on her chain to get going, to patrol our regular circuit of the heart of the town.

There is seldom any traffic; perhaps the steadfast jogger who lives about five miles from here. We wonder, the dog and I, if she jogs all the way to the Panhandle, or parks nearby and then circumnavigates the lap.

My mood is maternal, vigilant. Our neighbors are still tucked in snoozing, and this walk/watch, as well as a purifying start to a day, assures me that all is well in my town. We briskly parade the Panhandle, overseeing the seasons of the grasses, monitoring the arrival and departure of leaves, blossoms, nuts and berries, part-time West Tisburyites and then the crush of summer visitors.

From Music Street away from the town center, the houses become incidental; there are wild things, and at the center, always to the right, the ancient Whiting farm, its contours tempered by centuries of grazing sheep. The kids call the barn Fort Moon. We circle back to town, come upon the old farmhouse, where it is said a trunk in the attic is affixed with stickers from the Mayflower crossing. The house was built by Josiah Standish, the son of Myles, and their descendants are still in residence. In the early 1980's the farmhouse operated as a bed and breakfast but it was too invasive, and the refurbished house sits ready to shelter more generations of this venerable family. In old West Tisbury, history stays in place.

Much of the town's genealogy lies there in the graveyard, where salt-weather has blurred the loving inscriptions about sailors lost in storms, forty-niners lost on their way west.

One winter day about 30 years ago, the town handyman was assigned to dig a grave. The winter was harsh, the frozen ground relentless. So the handyman went to find a helper, offering his friend a bottle of whisky for sharing the task. The friend was grateful for the offer of gainful employment and the two returned to the dig. Before long, the diggers decided that the ground was so hard, they had better fortify themselves with a little advance in salary. They took a drink and continued to dig. The warming effects were so beneficial the workmen nibbled at the bottle, between hacks at the hard ground, until the bottle was empty. The town employee felt so selfish about consuming half of his friend's pay that he retrieved his own bottle from the floor of his truck, and they continued to dig.

It got dark. The handyman's wife began to worry about his whereabouts and called the police, who as they approached the blackness of the graveyard, heard merry singing. They found the two workmen, two shovels, and two empty bottles at the bottom of a nine-foot hole in the ground. It seems that when the diggers reached the soft loose sand under the frozen soil, they continued to shovel with such determination they didn't realize how deep they were. They were unable to climb out of their pit, and the police had to fetch a ladder for their release.

The dog and I continue around the Parsonage Pond, whose slopes are swift for sledding and whose calm shallow waters

When perfect weather elements permit, Parsonage Pond provides the best outdoor skating on the Island.

dle on the store's porch. The store looks handsomer in cedar singles than its asbestos siding of a previous generation. Inside, the locals complain between courses that the soup nowadays has too many herbs, not enough meat. But uniform in their timeless fashions, down jackets, plaid flannel shirts, Levi's, hammer holsters, and a pickup truck with a faithful hound, they take lunch daily and coffee breaks stretching from Labor Day through Memorial Day. They complain that the store has gone pretentious; they can't find a decent shovel or a brick of frozen squash. The freezer has been replaced by Majolica ware from Italy, little wooden toys from Germany. Not entirely. The store is still the kernel of the heart, the local source of sliced bread and six penny nails.

John Alley's first memory of the store is standing next to his father, allowed to work the big silver cash register. He says he got to push the buttons before his father cranked it. "You had to add everything up first on a paper bag and push in the numbers and crank it around a couple of times, then the drawer popped open."

He remembers a hulking black two-

provide the best skating rink in town. This is the steepest climb of our constitutional. We huff up the hill, around the bend to Alley's General Store, where from eight to five most any non-summer day, the locals hang out as they have for six or seven generations.

At this unsullied hour *The Boston Globe* has been unloaded in a tight bun-

The morning team gathers at Alley's.

184

door safe and a rolltop desk and kerosene stove attached to a black pipe that crossed the ceiling and spanned the two rooms that divided the store. The store stayed open until seven in the evening because people picked up their mail after work and stuck around to share the news. Now it shuts down at five, and the town seals tight until daylight.

When the post office moves, it will mean a major surgical bypass for the heart of West Tisbury. The new post office may move to the site of the Morris Rosenthal house, across from the fair grounds. Morris Rosenthal was a retired doctor known for his uneven driving skills. "He didn't back up none too good," John Alley says. When Morris came to Alley's to fetch his mail, his neighbors left a wide berth around his car. Albion Alley loved to recall the day he was on the steps of the store when Morris arrived for his mail. Morris got in his car and pushed the accelerator to the floorboard before shifting into reverse. As he let out the clutch, the black Falcon charged backwards and Morris ran straight into the car wash, now the garden center and croissant shop called Back Alley's. There was, swears John Alley, a scar in the stucco until Back Alley's came to be. Morris leaped out of his car and shouted "Who the hell put THAT there?" about the well-established car wash.

Across the street, where police chief George Manter says he learned how to smoke by blowing corn silk in the summer fields, live Tom Maley's capricious rolypoly dancers, pushing 30 some of them, frozen in performance in the old cornfield that is now the Field Gallery. Jane Brehm, the widow of another artist, used to call them "critters." For those who live nearby, an endless roll of laughter continues through the daylight, through the summer, into the winter, as visitors with cameras imitate the spirited poses. There are few sunny winter week-

One of Tom Maley's eyecatching sculptures at the Field Gallery provides a perfect playground.

ends without down-bundled burlesque going on out there, pirouetting for snapshots between bouts of helpless laughter.

The church is the metaphysical center, even for non-believers, a pristine formal Yankee squared-off untarnished clapboard symbol, its bell reminding the town of the hour, and in so doing, jarring the winter silence and setting the neighborhood dogs to howling.

Across Music Street the overcrowded town hall was, not so many years ago, the overcrowded schoolhouse. In the 1950's when Helen O'Donnell was the teacher, the school taught through fourth grade and each row of seats contained a grade. By 1974 the school moved halfway to Vineyard Haven and at the advent of the 1990's, has 300 kids to enlighten.

Next door—and what a torture it must have been—is the fair grounds. Back in the 40's the fair was held in September and included amusements developed by local people, George Magnuson or Everett Howell, who set up games of chance with triangles of weighted milk bottles and balls borrowed from the kids.

The fair moved to August, became the meridian of up-Island summer, the carneys moved in, the off-Island booths, blinking beckoning colored lights. In the

The ubiquitous John Alley.

West Tisbury police chief, George Wanter.

185

The focal point of a frenetic August is the Agricultural Fair.

186

middle 50's, Colbert's Fiesta came to operate the midway, with a merry-go-round, a Ferris wheel, the Octopus, the Mixer, the Chairplane, kiddie rides, all.

An aerialist called the Great Lamarr set up poles and taut ropes on what is now the town hall playground basketball court. Lamarr's first year, in the early 60's, the whole fair was brought to a halt. The music on the PA system stopped. The merry-go-round and the Ferris wheel stopped spinning mid-ride. The PA system announced that the Great Lamarr would attempt his Leap for Life, accompanied by the staccato excitement of the Sabre Dance. Fairgoers moved en masse to watch. The second summer, the music stopped but the rides kept turning. The third summer, nothing stopped, Lamarr simply did his Leap for Life without fanfare for anyone who passed nearby. Lamarr stopped coming to West Tisbury.

For three days in the third week of August, West Tisbury is sin city. Lock up your daughters, your pets, take your laundry off the line. The worst of the sins is strangers parking on your lawn, leaving behind their ketchup-stained food wrappings. The best of the sins is sheer exhilaration we can't help but feel, like three straight days of Christmas.

But that pinnacle and the throngs are half a year away. Right now, while the dog and I complete our walk, the quickening wind is a cold companion on our deserted street.

Eileen Maley was born and raised in Canada, and has worked for newspapers and magazines in Toronto and Vancouver before moving to winterless Australia. She kept heading west and landed in West Tisbury. She had lived on Music Street with her husband Timothy Maley since 1974. She is the features editor of The Martha's Vineyard Times.

A look towards the village of West Tisbury.

The Keith Farm barn in Chilmark.

Quitsa Pond overlook.

Chilmark;
Two Words Is Not Enough

BY NANCY SLONIM ARONIE

When my Eastern European Jewish grandmother met my husband for the first time, she said, "I have two voids for dat boy: vondaful."

In 1971, when my husband and I first came to the Vineyard for a weekend I turned to him and said, "I have two voids for dis Island . . ."

It was spring and we rode our bikes from Vineyard Haven to Gay Head and when we got to Beetlebung Corner hundreds of daffodils danced in the cold April chill. *Where have you been*, they whispered. I waited at the crossroads for my husband, who had the bad bike. Where *have* I been, I wondered.

We took a left on State Road and when I got to that woodframe Victorian house on the hill I took a mental photograph of the pale yellow Painted Lady. And when we got to the lighthouse I snapped another shot. Rust and violet ribbon candy cliffs melting into a navy blue sea. On our way back to town we stopped at Alley's, and I remember the bulletin board being as delicious as the hot chocolate we sipped as we sat on the porch blowing clouds of steamy breath into damp salt air. It was perfect.

Yoga workshop on the beach 6 A.M.

**Lamaze group forming,
call Heather**

**Macrobiotic cooking lessons
in my home**

Where *have* I been I said out loud. Did they put these notices up for me? When they saw me rolling by, did they say, "Quick here comes Nance—put up the new age stuff."

I had missed the sixties. During Woodstock I was fluffing my Marimeko pillows and tossing romaine greens in my matching Dansk salad bowls. I was traveling while other women were tripping; I was having babies while other women were having hallucinations; I was playing Chutes and Ladders while they were playing flutes and guitars. I was determined to make up the electric koolaid acid test I had missed.

We began returning to the Vineyard offseason twice a year. Every fall and spring we would discover a new trail, a new bike path, a new way to eat bluefish. Then when my son Josh turned seven, he and I began running the Mother's Day Road Race. It became our annual coastal pil-

A peek behind roadside shrubs reveals one of Chilmark's most dramatic homes.

Keeping in touch with Island happenings at Alley's.

The Chilmark Store—a gathering place for weary bikers, summer people, and for Up-Island natives who don't mind paying higher prices in order to avoid Down-Island traffic.

grimage. We were hooked on the Island and any excuse we could find to come back we used—a wedding in October, a baby naming in February, the Thrift Shop fashion show in March.

Finally we rented a place in the summer. And then finally, we were able to buy our own place. The closing was in late November and on our way out of the lawyer's office I turned to my husband and said, "I would love to spend the month of January here." And then I

wheeled around to see who had spoken such words. It was not something I had even thought about.

My husband said, "Do it."

"Who's gonna do carpool and dentist appointments and soccer practice?" I asked.

"I will," he said.

So on New Year's Day, with no wood, and a wood stove and an unwinterized cabin in Chilmark, I took my own mini Outward Bound, "The-Vineyard-in-January" course.

The winter Vineyard was white that stayed white. Listening to the scallop report from New Bedford on WMVY, sipping blackberry tea from a yorsteit glass, watching birds peck at my kitchen window, reading in the attic of the Chilmark library, I had one of the most nourishing experiences of my life. My pipes froze, my husband tuned into the orthodontist, orthopedic, opthomologist parts of our kids lives, I got a chance to be alone for 30 days, and I discovered plumbing is not one of my priorities.

The first summer was the best. None of us knew anyone, so we clung and hung together. Afternoons we'd spend in the hammock, munching on popcorn, my two babies cradled in my arms, making up "to be continued" stories and reading *Swiftly Tilting Planet* and *The Chronicles of Narnia*.

The second summer all the people, who had politely not called the first summer, called. They arrived with their Entemanns offerings and Haagen Dazs house warmings and they insisted on The Ocean Club for dinner. By Labor Day, I was craving quiet in my own head and broccoli in my own house.

The next summer my kids got jobs. Running into the Chilmark store and watching Josh, then 11, weighing grapes and bagging bananas I thought I had died and gone to heaven. And then going down to Vineyard Haven and sneaking behind Gannon and Benjamin, hiding on the side of a huge wooden yacht and staring in proud disbelief at my baby (Dan, nine) drilling holes for pegs, I *knew* I had died and gone to heaven.

Each season has had its own exquisiteness, its own magic, and each fall back in Connecticut I'd think "Yup, this one was the best." The year my husband entered the tiniest kite in the kite contest; the August 6th trips to Nomans with Barbara and Zach; the night my 17 year old, who at 14 wrote an essay for his school literary magazine entitled "What a guru told my mother" (disclaiming anything spiritual), invited *me* to see Ram Dass at the Whaling Church; slicing and dicing onions by the thousands for Lyn and Jules Worthington and their prize winning Tempura booth; moaning appropriately by the bedside of one of Charlie Parton's Halloween scalpel victims; taking my first private ice skating lesson at the arena from Sascha Wlodyka while James Taylor sang solo over the loudspeakers exclusively to us—the only skaters there; doing "doggies" in the 90 degree heat on the Community Center floor; crying and laughing at the talent show; running the

Chilmark Road Race; preparing my speech and fixing my sweaty curls for Peter Simon's inevitable photograph, "She tried to run fast but alas she was LAST." These are among millions of precious Vineyard memories.

Now that the planet is tilting faster than the speed of life, the daffodils no long whisper, they bellow, "Two words is not enough."

Nancy Slonim Aronie is a freelance writer and radio commentator who lives in West Hartford, Connecticut. Her stories have appeared in Good Housekeeping, Leers, New England Monthly, *to name a few. She is a regular columnist for* The Martha's Vineyard Times *and may be heard on National Public Radio's "All Things Considered."*

The annual Chilmark Road Race start line on Middle Road—good competition and a chance to renew summer acquaintances at the finish line.

*Many parts of the Vineyard remain unspoiled despite—and perhaps due to—
contradictory measures controlling development.*

The Big Picture

BY DOUGLAS CABRAL

I sailed to the Vineyard on the little double ended cutter that was also my home. It was July Fourth weekend, 1970. And the Vineyard then was not the Vineyard we know today. At anchor near the corner of the old steamboat wharf in Vineyard Haven, the one with the big grey-shingled building sprawling all over the end of it, I could look ashore, and there was no Black Dog.

The Black Dog formed first in the imaginations of two men, Robert Douglas, who owned the beachfront land and a pile of yellow pine timbers for which he had no immediate use in mind, and Alan Miller, a speedy genius of a builder. Douglas thought the Island needed a good restaurant, a chowder house where folks could sit around a wood fire all winter and swap lies. Miller thought so too, but mostly he had a gleam in his eye about those tremendous timbers. He had a vision.

In the Vineyard of 1970-1971, from vision to construction was a quick passage —no building permits, no conservation-this, or board of health-that. To start building the Black Dog, Alan just chose a spot and started to dig. The bones of that stalwart, now-familiar structure began rising a few months after I came to live here.

There was no zoning then on Martha's Vineyard, and there were fewer arguments. The era of bitter argument began in earnest on April 1972, with the introduction in Congress of the Islands Trust Bill, also called the Kennedy Bill, after Sen. Edward M. Kennedy. Islanders have been scrapping with increasing viciousness ever since.

If you stroll among the piney woods along the shore of Lake Tashmoo, the air is spicey, not leaden the way summer breezes often are elsewhere, and there's a barn owl who hunts the woods; you can see ospreys fishing just offshore, there are highbush blueberries and lady's slippers. But as remarkable as anything else you may observe are the fireplugs.

These fireplugs offer mute, stubborn, witness to the way we fight. There are 106 thickly wooded, gently rolling acres here, uninhabited for years, now sprinkled with fireplugs and excavations, and some fancy triplexes, parking areas and tennis courts. Developer Joseph Chira installed the fireplugs and dug the foundations before he lost the right to cluster 150 summer homes in these woods. He would not give up or modify his plan, and his neighbors would not give up their opposition. After more than two years of hearings and lawsuits and charges and counter-charges, foreclosure proceedings by the investors brought the $1.5 million dream to an end. The development known as Tashmoo Woods, eighty or so dwellings, is the work of Chira's 1980's successor.

In 1974, Senator Kennedy held an Islandwide hearing at the Tisbury School concerning the future of Island growth.

It is ironic that the development of Martha's Vineyard and the proliferation of protective regulation and zoning have matched one another stride for stride and battle for battle. While Vineyarders blistered one another over twenty fractious years, lot after lot was created following the blueprint laid down by zoning, and building after building sprang up.

A 1971 report on the environment of the Vineyard and its future by the engineering firm Metcalf & Eddy warned that "one of the few bastions of rural environmental splendor in the United States, faces clear and present danger from despoilers. . . .The next five years are critical. If a definite and well-ordered program of preventive medicine is not undertaken immediately or within the next five years, by 1975 the Vineyard will undoubtedly have contracted environmental terminal cancer."

The report was wrong. The preventive medicine, the rules and regulations, the name calling, and the raging legal battles did little to prevent or channel growth, but the symptoms of terminal growth disease continue to be mild.

The passing of Joseph Chira's scheme was followed shortly by the collapse of Strock Enterprises in the face of the fledgling Martha's Vineyard Commission. Established in 1974 by the Massachusetts legislature to stave off the genuinely conservationist Kennedy Bill, and charged with planning and regulating growth across the Island's six towns, the 21-member, slimly financed and understaffed organization faced its first great challenge with Strock. And the two sides went to court. Litigation was the chief tool of growth control until, in March of 1977, the Supreme Court of Massachusetts found for the Martha's Vineyard Commission and against Strock's plans, which contemplated some 250 building lots and 507 acres of woods and meadows bordering Sengekontacket Pond. This was an enormous subdivision plan for Martha's Vineyard where, as late as 1972, only one of its six constituent towns had zoning and subdivision control laws on its books.

Strock lost, and the Vineyard gained, not wilderness exactly, but lovely Farm Neck Golf Course and its sprinkling of lavish fairway homes.

But time—and interest rates—have taken some of the fight out of the developers, and the faces of the planners have changed. Now, it is not to court but to the bargaining table that developers and townspeople often go. Of course, houses still are built, and commercial property developed at a late 1980's rate that's numbing, but it is impossible to decide if either side wins. In dealing with developers of the 1980's, the Martha's Vineyard Commission and the town planning and conservation agencies stretch their legal powers to the limits—to lower potential housing density, to preserve the rural appearance of roadsides, to protect the groundwater from contamination, to preserve ancient ways, to provide for the housing needs of young Islanders of modest means, and to establish growth rates. In every instance the community must settle for less than would be ideal. And so must the developers.

And the debate has reached kick and gouge proportions. The Vineyard's failure to agree on what it wants to be and how it wants to grow has meant that perceived development threats are met head on, ad hoc, and the most strident, most personal attack may prevail.

In Chilmark, protection of ancient Tea Lane led the town to increase minimum lot size for land near the road from three to five acres. Julia Sturges and Eleanor Pearlson, Chilmark residents affected dramatically by the change, fought to no avail among their neighbors on the town meeting floor, but they won in court. The court found that other, less drastic means, might have been invoked to improve and protect the road.

In Tisbury, Edward Redstone's plan to build a new Martha's Vineyard National Bank headquarters and a supermarket at the site of the old Nobnocket Garage near the Tashmoo overlook provoked such a partisan battle, that Redstone was attacked personally and repeatedly, not only by individuals, but by the *Vineyard Gazette*, and supporters of his project were attacked as well. Years after the bat-

Eleanor Pearlson and Julia Sturges plead their case at the yearly town meeting in Chilmark.

tle, scar tissue has not fully formed. And this was a project, needed by the bank, needed by the market, in compliance with town and regional rules, and successful in gaining regulatory approval. It was beaten on political and personal grounds.

Many who fought in the Kennedy Bill and the Strock and Chira wars have retired now to their gardens or the clam flats. It's waders and trowels now, not injunctions and briefs.

Bargaining often occurs now between government and developer. Architect Sam Dunn's plan for the Tisbury Market Place business center along low-lying Beach Road is an example. The property, owned until its bankruptcy by Strock Enterprises, occupies the marshy borders of the Lagoon Pond. Several buildings in varying states of disrepair saw only marginal use over the past decade. Dunn's plan was rejected by the town conservation commission and in other towns. It was too big, and the septic system contemplated to serve the new construction, it was argued by environmentalists, would not prevent rapid pollution of the Lagoon. Months and months went by while Dunn was out of business and the town conservation commission waited for the next shoe to drop. But with the help of some nearly anonymous, quietly influential outsiders, Dunn and the conservation commission got together. The project went forward, but phased over time, with its progress limited by the results of regular ground and pond water sampling from wells the developer was obliged to drill.

The question is: what does the community want? How do you grow according to master plans which do not exist, or exist but are forgotten? Into the void flows frustration, and anger. We fight instead of plan.

Perhaps, as some believe, the community standards of easy sociability, small-scale harmonious growth patterns, flexible, tolerant lifestyles, and open swing-from-the-ankles town meeting politics tacitly inform the judgments of Vineyard planners and town leaders. That's not what I have found.

The Vineyard, some say, may look different here and there from what it was twenty years ago, but at heart it is the same. To me, the landscape often seems less changed than the quality of debate.

A former managing editor of the Vineyard Gazette, *Douglas Cabral took over as editor of* The Martha's Vineyard Times *in 1985 and has seen the new paper gain in stature ever since. His controversial editorials never fail to arouse emotion, but sometimes point the way to new solutions. He lives with his ever expanding family in Chilmark.*

Christmas time at the Tisbury Marketplace.

Time passages.

The Brustein expanse.

Vineyard Passage

BY ROBERT BRUSTEIN

I spent my first summer on Martha's Vineyard three months after I was married. During our second summer on the island, my wife was pregnant. By our third summer, following the birth of our son, Daniel, we had taken up residence in the house we had bought on Lambert's Cove. Fourteen years later, at the start of our fourteenth summer, I buried my wife's ashes under a maternal beech tree near the garden she loved and tended. And in August of our twenty-second summer, my son's son, Maxwell, was born in Martha's Vineyard hospital. Birth and death, place and family, are inextricable on this island, and we measure our years by the passage of our summers.

I have lived in many cities, both in this country and abroad. I was born and raised in New York. I have endured thirteen years in New Haven and enjoyed eleven in Cambridge. I have spent only two precious months out of each of the past twenty-seven years on Martha's Vineyard. Nevertheless this Island! has been the one geographical constant in the hearts of a family that always valued emotional constancy—it is our root, our base, our home.

In the midst of this pastoral stability, however, there is the inevitable pattern of change, and in my seasonal role of summer squire, traversing my land as an excuse to avoid my work, I often contemplate the alterations in nature and architecture that have marked these years on the Vineyard. The original A frame of our early-nineteenth-century house has now been alphabetically joined by L's and H's, as we added new bedrooms, a porch, and a dining room to accommodate our growing family. The bedroom was mistakenly built over our well, and we had to cut a hole in the floor for access. The willow we planted some distance away when we first purchased the house had to be removed when it began to threaten the water pipes in our new kitchen. The sassafras grove has multiplied like the weed it is; and the shiny myrtle cover spreads over the land like a counterpane. In my walks, I frequently come upon some token of things past—a piece of the toy lawn mower my toddler son employed to imitate his father's labors, a remnant of the stone wall moved some fifty feet north when we acquired another acre.

How curious this Vineyard life has been, then, as if we had spent here one long summer of twenty-seven years duration, during which the children had grown, close friends had died, bodies and faces had aged, architecture expanded, vegetation increased. A long summer of time in which, year after year, I was able to renew strong relationships with friends rarely seen in winter, discover new fishing holes, improve and disimprove my tennis, watch the *Diabolique* go to the bottom in a late summer storm, replace it with a fast Formula Thunderbird for the sake of my water-skiing son, watch the sea grass accumulate on the hull, being too lazy to scrape it off, live with a radio that received but couldn't transmit, drink a little more, eat a little less, and compare the summer's weather with that of decades past, old enough to talk of its deterioration.

What else has changed? The placement of the clams in Tashmoo pond—but not my pleasure in digging for them. Indeed, I have never fully understood why clamming in Tashmoo has always constituted the single most delicious activity of my Vineyard summer—even more appealing than those joyous laugh-filled doubles games at the Yacht Club and Seven Gates, or that first brisk dip into the July waters of South Beach when you emerge from the surf with the sun kissing the salt on your body, or, on a really humid day, the exquisite fresh water embrace of

Uncle Seth's Pond, swimming past the eager children to the place where turtles sun themselves on rocks. Yes, I do understand the appeal of clamming. It is my single opportunity to be alone with my island and contemplate its startling beauty.

Let me tell you about it. I start out from my mooring in Tashmoo Pond and—after a fast run to West Chop and back to charge my fickle battery—return to the channel, cutting the engine almost to an idle. The current pushes against the slight forward movement of the channel waters. I throw an anchor on Milton Gordon's beach, and with a yellow plastic bucket in hand, tied to my waist with a frayed rope, go to my secret place for clams. As I squat in the water at low tide, I can just see the osprey feeding its young, the gulls wheeling over Tashmoo beach, a flock of geese in flight honking and flapping in perfect formation. Warmed by the sun, I feel through the cold sand with my heels and toes, scratch under the muck, find nothing. A crab pinches my fingers and I draw away in pain. I am scrabbling the bottom now with my ten fingers and my ten toes, moving back and forth through the water, hips swaying in a Tashmoo hula. Noth-

ing. Can it be that the accursed professional clammers with their rakes and gadgets, have taken all the bivalves?

A hard object responds to my touch—a good-sized cherrystone. There is a tiny clam nearby it—I heave it into the deeper waters of the pond. I cut my finger on an open shell and suck the blood—a common hazard of clamming. In an hour, I have collected enough quahaugs for soup and enough cherrystones for an appetizer on the half-shell for a party of eight, but I come upon another nest of clams. Is it a family? Do they form schools like fish? I swear to stop when I find four more, but I break my promise when I come upon five in one small area. I understand gambling now, and acquisition, and remember how hard it was to cut down on cigars. I am in the grip of a habit and I love it. My knees are beginning to buckle, my back aches. I stop to contemplate the sky, the ducks, the gently purring waters. Finally, I wrest myself away and carry my catch over the sharp rocks to my boat. Returning to the mooring, I take a slow quiet cruise to the end of the pond, near State Road, looking at rocking boats, geese nesting in a cove, leaping fish. It is the memory I retain most vividly in the long winter to come.

The Vineyard, then, is my world of growth and stability, representing at once the capacity for change and the capacity for permanence. It is the single season when work and pleasure, society and isolation, community and privacy conjoin in perfect harmony. T. S. Eliot's lady measured out her life in coffee spoons. I, much luckier, have measured out my own in Vineyard summers. The sound of the West Chop foghorn, the barking of a far-away dog, the topping of trees in Mohu, the spacious inviting expanse of my neighbor's meadow, the goofy pigeon-toed quail scurrying in panic when I come up our dusty driveway, the wet-eyed deer that meets my gaze for a moment before bounding into the woods, the chattering birds on the roof, the mouse droppings that inevitably appear on the stove when the house is left vacant for more than three days, the phallic mushrooms that bloom near my study after a night of hard rain, the memories, the ghosts, the strange sounds in the night—these and much more are the images of my passage, the token of my sojourn on this paradise of summer, this Island of change.

Robert Brustein, when not beating Mike Wallace on the tennis court, is artistic director of the American Repertory Theatre at Harvard University, where he also serves as Professor of English. He is the drama critic for The New Republic *and lives in Cambridge, Massachusetts with his son Daniel and grandson Max, who is a native Vineyarder.*

Uncle Seth's Pond.

Darkness and light on Vineyard Sound.

Island Trilogy

BY CARLY SIMON

Fisherman's Song

In a pine forest
Cooler than the rest of the Island
Lives a young fisherman
With eyes like the sea
He built his own boat
And made his own cabin
But he's broken the heart
   of the likes of me.

Now you must understand
He made me a promise
There were secrets we shared
We planted a tree
We lived in his cabin
I fished along side of him
I fell under the spell
Of his sorcery.

When he cast me adrift
At the end of the summer
It was not for another
But his own privacy
I fell apart like a rose
But the scent of my longing
Remains and it weeps
Like an old willow tree.

At night when it's still
With a yellow moon rising
And his candle is snuffed
And he's deep in a dream
I move like a cat
And crawl into his window
And lie down beside him
In a golden moon beam.

The smell of his skin
Is just like the summer
When our love was as fresh
As the grass in the fields
And ever so softly
I kiss his eyelids
Before slipping away
My secret concealed.

Though I'm in it alone
I'm still in it in love
And love can be lonely
Like a sweet melody
But just maybe he feels me
Like a whisper inside him
Like an angel beside him
Keeping him company.

Never Been Gone

The wind is coming up strong and fast
And the moon is smiling on me
Miles from nowhere
So small at last
In between the sky and sea.

I'm bound for the Island
The tide is with me
I think I can make it by dawn
It's night on the ocean and I'm going
    home
And it feels like I've never,
    never been gone.

Seagulls cry and the hills are green
And my friends are waiting for me
Great ambition is all a dream
Let me drown my pride in the sea.

I'm bound for the Island
The tide is with me
I think I can make it by dawn
It's night on the ocean and I'm going
    home
And it feels like I've never,
    never been gone.

We Just Got Here

There are a few new freckles on your shoulders
    The hammock swings lower
And touches the grass
The apples are ripe and the corn is past
Everyone says summer goes by so fast
And we just got here.

I can hardly believe it but it's ended
The beach is a haze
And old love is a ghost
Hugo is twisting his way up the Coast
If you blew out to sea I'd love you the most
And we just got here.

Nostalgia you fake
You bittersweet ache
The time that you take
Could make another heart whole
Could the truth be
I won't really see
How much I love you . . . 'til it's over.

The two of us left here alone in the house
You bleed the pipes
I bring in the plants
Put our faces in place for September's dance
If you're willing, I'm willing
To take one more chance . . .
And we just got here.

Carly Simon began her musical career singing with her sister, Lucy, at the Mooncusser Café, a folk music club on Circuit Avenue in 1962, and moved here semi-permanently in 1971. Despite her dislike for live performances, she has managed a few memorable appearances here, including the No Nukes Festival in 1978 in Chilmark, a gig at the club she co-founded, The Hot Tin Roof in 1982, and an HBO special staged in Gay Head in 1987. She collaborated with Vineyard artist Margot Datz on the recently published children's book, Amy The Dancing Bear *(Doubleday). On the way is another children's book as well as a collection of semi-autobiographical short stories. Carly summers in Tisbury with occasional retreats to Menemsha with her husband James Hart and her children, Sally and Ben.*